THE WAY OF TRUTH
IN THE PRESENT AGE

THE WAY OF TRUTH
IN THE PRESENT AGE

Edited by

Craig M. Gay and C. Pete Molloy

REGENT COLLEGE PUBLISHING
VANCOUVER, BRITISH COLUMBIA

The Way of Truth in the Present Age
Copyright ©1999 Regent College Publishing

First edition 1999
Published by Regent College Publishing, an imprint of the Regent College Bookstore, 5800
University Blvd., Vancouver, B.C. Canada V6T 2E4

Sections of the article, "Being True in the Present Age" are taken from Craig M. Gay, *The Way
of the (Modern) World: Or Why it's Tempting to Live as if God Doesn't Exist* (Grand Rapids, MI:
Eerdmans-Regent, 1998).

Printed in the United States of America

Canadian Cataloguing in Publication Data

Main entry under the title:

The way of truth in the present age

Papers presented at the Western Theological Conference held in Vancouver, B.C., February
1998.
Includes bibliographical references and index.
ISBN 0-88865-436-7 (Canada)
ISBN 1-57383-132-8 (U.S.)

1. Truth (Christian Theology)—Congresses.   2. Postmodernism—Religious aspects—
Congresses. I. Gay, Craig M.   II. Molloy, C. Pete.   III. Western Theological Conference
(1998: Vancouver, B.C.)

BT50.W39 1999   231'.042   C99-910822-0

Contributors

Craig M. Gay is Associate Professor of Interdisciplinary Studies at Regent College.

David Lyle Jeffrey teaches at Augustine College in Ottawa and is Emeritus Professor of English Literature at the University of Ottawa.

C. Pete Molloy is a graduate student at Regent College and a researcher at the Fraser Institute in Vancouver, B.C.

J. I. Packer is Board of Governors' Professor of Theology at Regent College and the director of the College's Anglican Studies Programme.

Barbara Pell is Professor of English at Trinity Western University in Langley, B.C.

Michael Treschow is Professor of English Literature at Okanagan University College in Kelowna, British Columbia.

Loren Wilkinson is Professor of Interdisciplinary Studies and Philosophy at Regent College.

Contents

Foreword

The Prayer Book Society of Canada has as its essential rationale the propagation of the concept of doctrine in devotion. The Society is, therefore, committed to a sound, historic, biblical, Trinitarian and incarnational faith and to the expression of that faith in the public worship of the Church and the private devotion of her members. The Society believes that the classic Anglican way of Common Prayer is a sure foundation for such faith and worship.

In our times the classic Anglican way—and the historic faith it expounds—have fallen into disuse, even contempt. The Society is called upon to mount a significant educational effort in order to re-awaken contemporary Christians and non-Christians alike to their loss, their need and the means ready to hand to remedy both.

The Society's educational work is carried on at several levels. One is the support and promotion of regular theological conferences across the country at which major contemporary theological issues are publicly explored by top-flight minds. The Society's first Western Theological Conference was held at Kelowna, British Columbia in August 1995 on the topic of the Theology of Prayer. The response demonstrated a definite desire for such conferences and the second was organized for Vancouver in February 1998. The papers for this second conference are now presented to the wider church and to Canadian society in this present volume by Regent College Publishing. The Prayer Book Society of Canada is much indebted to Regent College Publishing and the editors, Craig M. Gay and C. Pete Molloy for their enormous assistance, and for the access given to so much larger an audience then the Society could hope to reach on its own.

For the Society I would like to say a special word of thanks to the contributors to the Vancouver Conference who gave their time and energy so generously in the production and delivery of the papers that now follow. Their joint and several contributions to the Anglican way will, I hope, be widely broadcast through this volume.

—Graham Eglington,
National Director,
The Prayer Book Society of Canada

Introduction

Perhaps we should not be surprised that the idea of Truth has come under fire in contemporary culture. Truth with a capital "T," after all, has never been easy to affirm; for as the old churchly phrase put it so aptly: "the world wants to be deceived." Still, the forcefulness and vehemence with which recent advocates of pluralism, multiculturalism, and other "isms" falling under the larger rubric of "postmodernism" have attacked the notion of Truth is unsettling, even if not completely surprising. If, instead of Truth, there is finally only a cacophony of "truths" relative to the particular desires and circumstances of individuals and groups, as is being so boldly asserted these days, then what, besides simple coincidence and/or coercion, can ever be expected to bring people together? To what, if not to Justice, is one supposed to appeal in the event of having been wronged? And for what, beyond the satisfaction and legitimation of one's own desires, is one to seek in attempting to live an examined life? And, most importantly, how can today's resolute denial of the possibility of Truth ever be squared with the call to believe on the One who says "I am the Way, the Truth, and the Life"?

These are troubling questions. And yet in spite of the fact that it is impossible even to begin to answer without relying on something like the idea of Truth, postmodernism's beguiling skepticism is popular and getting more so all the time. While the repudiation of truth appears to have surfaced first in academic and intellectual circles, it has become an increasingly common presumption in popular culture and, indeed, in ordinary discourse. What can possibly account for this? What lies behind postmodernism's triumphant, and yet apparently barren and self-destructive incredulity? Does it stem from the legitimate grievances of those—women perhaps, adherents of non-Christian religions, the colonized—whose only experience of Christian civilization came in the form of a stultifying and oppressive "modernity"? In this connection, to the extent that a secularized commitment to truth is held to lie at the heart of modern development, then perhaps postmodern agnosticism and/or atheism is best understood as a kind of understandable—if misguided—plea for freedom and for genuinely human meaning in the context of secular modernity's unfreedom and soullessness. Or is postmodern skepticism simply an expression of licentiousness and, ultimately, of what the Bible calls "lawlessness"? How we answer these questions, of course, will have a lot to do with whether we think that Christians must somehow hold out against the contemporary drift towards the postmodern or whether we believe it better to try to make a kind of strategic alliance with postmodernism for the sake of overcoming secular modernity. Obviously, a great many questions remain to be answered.

In February of 1998, six Canadian Anglican scholars paused to consider the various challenges of postmodernism at a Western Theological Conference entitled "The Way of Truth in the Present Age," sponsored by the Prayer Book Society of Canada and held at St. John's (Shaughnessy) Church in Vancouver. All six addressed the problems associated with affirming Christianity today in a culture that has become increasingly skeptical of all truth claims. Although written within the context of the Anglican Communion and directed primarily to an Anglican audience, the addresses have been published together in this volume as they concern matters that are of pressing relevance to all Christians today.

J. I. Packer responds to the contemporary notion that all the world's religions are, in effect, pathways to divinity, and contends, to the contrary, that only Christian truth offers us "a map, diagram, and index of reality, and as such a doorway into it, realization of it, and a pathway through it."

Michael Treschow emphasizes the "comfort-able" quality of Christian truth and the enduring capacity of the Gospel of Jesus Christ

12

to comfort troubled souls and to bring peace and justice to the nations.

Barbara Pell suggests that although postmodernism's repudiation of truth is a philosophical and theological cul-de-sac, postmodern literary criticism nevertheless provides Christians with a powerful critique of modern secular humanism and important clues as to how Christian truth should be represented in contemporary culture.

Craig Gay contends that by adopting a fundamentally instrumental and manipulative attitude toward truth, the present age has effectively nullified the possibility of knowing the truth of the living God.

Loren Wilkinson submits that, in an intellectual climate in which the traditional Christian affirmation of the authority of Scripture tends to give offense, Christians can still fruitfully direct their contemporaries to the truth of a created order that has the power to pull us wordlessly, as it were, to where the word is made flesh.

And lastly, David Jeffery reminds us that we can only really know the truth to the extent that we are prepared to walk obedient before God, who alone is the Truth.

One final word of caution: Christian thinkers are currently arriving at a variety of different conclusions with respect to postmodernity's root proposition, which may explain why the essays represented here arrive at somewhat disparate, and at both more and less hopeful assessments of the postmodern situation, and each on the basis of biblical Christianity. You may find this perplexing, but hopefully you will also find it stimulating. For in spite of their differing perspectives, we believe that the essays offered in this volume represent precisely the kind of thoughtful Christian reflection that the present age calls for.

We gratefully acknowledge the permission of the Prayer Book Society of Canada to present the following essays. Proceeds from the sale of this volume will be contributed to the ongoing work of the Society. We would also like to thank Norah Johnston, Michael Treschow, and the organisers of the first Western Theological Conference, as well as the staff of St. John's (Shaughnessy) for their willingness to host this important event. Finally, we would like to acknowledge Dal Schindell and Rob Clements of *Crux* for their help in the editing and the preparation of the following material.

—Craig M. Gay and C. Pete Molloy
Regent College, Vancouver, B.C.

-1-

The Substance of Truth in the Present Age

J. I. Packer

This paper is offered as a contribution to our conference task of thinking out a Christian response to the postmodernity that surrounds us today. I said "Christian"; I meant "Christian." You might have expected me to say "Anglican," since we meet officially as Anglicans—right-wing Anglicans, some would call us—but the first thing I need, and want, to make clear is that to me, and I hope to you too, the word "Anglican" means purely, simply, and merely Christian. Surely we know that ever since the Reformation the essential Anglican claim, made first for the Church of England in England and then for the many units of Anglicanism worldwide that have been founded directly or indirectly from England, has been that Anglicanism is what C. S. Lewis, echoing Richard Baxter, called "mere Christianity"—that is to say, the historic apostolic faith free from both additions and subtractions; Christianity without trimmings, as we might put it; plain, straightforward, unadulterated Christianity according to the Scriptures and according to Jesus Christ our Lord. The primary evidence for this claim is the 39 Articles of 1562, the Prayer Book heritage from 1549 and 1552 through 1662 to 1962, and the writings of a long series of theologians from Cranmer, Jewel and Hooker to such as William Temple, Michael Ramsey and John Stott, all framed for us in Canada by the Solemn Declaration of 1893. I accept the claim fully, and address myself in the first instance to others who accept it too.

But I need to clarify my claim, or I shall be misunderstood as a denominational imperialist, which I trust I am not. When I say "Christianity," I do not mean just Christianity on paper; I mean Christianity as a going concern, a continuing corporate community of persons who know and love our Lord Jesus Christ as their Saviour, Master and Friend, who worship his Father in heaven as their Father in heaven, who seek to live in the power of the Holy Spirit, sanctifying all relationships by love, who see the world as the field where they must ever be working for God, and who have in their hearts the extending of Christ's kingdom as the passion of their lives. This is my understanding of "mere Christianity," and I define authentic Anglican identity—shall I say, authentic Anglican reality—in these terms. I do not question that apostolic Christianity has taken other forms beside historic Anglicanism; at this moment I am only saying that for me, and I hope for you, historic Anglicanism, thus viewed, is Christianity in one of its valid forms, so that any response to postmodernity that is worked out in authentically Anglican terms will be, precisely, a Christian response.

I need, I think, to clarify this in a further way. Like you (I imagine) I constantly meet sociological descriptions of present-day Anglicanism that assume the current state and processes of our communion are definitive of Anglican identity in a way that no appeal to our heritage can be. These accounts contrast "then" and "now" as if what Anglicanism is now has more of God and of God's authority than did any version of Anglicanism in the past or do any of the historic formulations that I have mentioned. We are invited to believe that the Holy Spirit leads the entire Anglican communion onward and upward all the time into an ever richer synthesis of diversities, so that our proper theological, moral, liturgical, and devotional task today is to mine and cash the many nuggets of gold that the novelties of this era are setting before us. We are encouraged, so we find, to look for a new theology, a new morality, and new forms of liturgy and spiritual life that somehow transcend and certainly leave behind what was there before. In this year leading up to Lambeth[1] '98, as in each year preceding each Lambeth in the second half of this fast-changing twentieth century, there has been much talk of this kind, and there will no doubt be more. I want to say to you quite explicitly that I think this evolutionary—indeed, revolutionary—way of understanding Anglicanism should be rejected. I see much of Western Anglicanism —Anglo-Anglicanism, as I prefer to call it—as being led by deviant academics, myopic ecclesiastics and journalistic loud-shouters into a measure of public apostasy, and my hope for Lambeth is that somehow the clearer and truer vision of Anglican leaders in black Africa and south-east Asia and South America may counter this Western decadence. It is in these terms, I believe, that we should be praying for Lambeth at the present time.

Putting the matter positively, I affirm that the biblical, evangelical, catholic and pastoral ideals of historic Anglicanism, anchored as they are in the patristic, medieval and Reformational heritages, constitute mainstream Christianity in a form distinguished only for richness of content and maturity of wisdom. I affirm that accounts of Anglicanism that represent it as essentially and desirably different from the rest of Christendom are on the wrong track. I identify one side of true Anglicanism, the Trinitarian, Christ-centered side, in the classic high church formula of one Bible, two Testaments, three Creeds, four Councils and five centuries, and I identify the other side of true Anglicanism, the redemptive, grace-and-salvation oriented side, as a heart-religion anchored in the attitudes and aspirations of Augustine, Cranmer, Hooker, Herbert, Baxter, Whitefield, Simeon, J. C. Ryle and William Temple—nine men who I think would have got on wonderfully well if we could have put them in a room together. As empirical Anglicanism in the West seems to me to be sadly like the man who named himself Legion, so ideal Anglicanism, as focused in our formularies and thought out and lived out by the heroes of our heritage, seems to me to be Christianity clothed and in its right mind, and I stand with the Essentials movement in supposing that to lead empirical Anglicanism back into the ways of ideal Anglicanism is the only way to lead it truly forward—and indeed, in Canada at any rate, to ensure even its survival. So now you see where I am coming from when I say that it is a Christian response to postmodernity that we as Anglicans must seek, and that to seek such a response is the most truly Anglican thing we can do.

Let us then attempt to do it.

What is postmodernity? It is popularly equated with a denial that there is any such thing as universal public truth, the idea being that there is only my truth and your truth, that which is true for me and that which is true for you, but there is no truth that is true for everybody. If that was all there was to it, it would not hard to dispose of. When a postmodernist started to tell you that there is no such thing as public universal truth, you would only need to ask him whether his assertion was being offered as a universal public truth or not. If he said yes, he would stand self-refuted, having denied his assertion by the very act of asserting it. If he said no, you would then tell him that his denial of the reality of public universal truth, which is on his view truth for him, is not truth for you, and that is that; you, as a believer in public universal truth, have a basis on which to try to persuade him that he is wrong, but he, as one who does not believe that what is true for anyone is true for everyone, has no basis for trying to persuade you he is right, and his attempt to do so is no more than an indefensible power play that has no claim to be taken seriously. (End of conversation.) Perhaps we already know that it is in those terms, that is, as an indefensible power play, that deconstructionists in the postmodern camp regularly write off persuasions to which they do not intend to yield. It is surely bracing to realize that sauce for the goose is also sauce for the gander, and that professional removers of motes from other people's eyes may yet have beams in their own.

Have we, then, said all that needs saying about postmodernity? Oh, no. Postmodern-*ity* is a mood and mindset among intellectuals in our Western society; it has become almost a fashion in our universities; it is a temper of disillusionment with, cynicism about, and reaction against, what is called modernity, and it has to be taken seriously. No skepticism of our own about the significance of intellectuals should keep us from doing that. Probably we are familiar with the pejorative use of the word "intellectual," the use found for instance in Paul Johnson's fun book, *Intellectuals*,[2] where an intellectual is one who pontificates about how others should live while being unable or unwilling to live that way himself. Perhaps we recall these lines of the late great W. H. Auden:

> To the man-in-the street, who, I'm
> sorry to say,
> Is a keen observer of life,
> The word "intellectual" suggests

straight away
A man who's untrue to his wife.[3]

But nothing we know about the personal phoniness of some intellectuals should divert us from seriously weighing what they say, when they articulate postmodernity just as when they verbalize other things; for intellectuals have insight and influence, they write what many read, and as university teachers and literary lions they are very much society's opinion-makers. We ignore them at our peril. I ask, then: how are we to understand the postmodernity professed by so many Western intellectuals? And I offer the following answer to my question.

For something like two hundred years, ever since the so-called Enlightenment first darkened Western minds through the influence of men like Rousseau and Kant and Jefferson and the theorists of the French Revolution, the cultural and educational establishments took for granted that man's mind was the measure of all things and truth and value were always and only discerned by reason working on the basis of observation and experiment. Reason, thus used, was called scientific, and the conclusions of scientific reason were made the lodestar for organizing all human life. Optimistically assuming that everything can be improved by planning and technology and will in any case sooner or later evolve into something better, modernity for two centuries sought to shape society through industrial development, social engineering, urbanization, education, and various forms of wealth creation. This process was expected to bring health, harmony and happiness to all the world, but the unmistakable witness of our barbaric, tribalized twentieth century is that it has totally failed to do so and totally lacks resources for ever doing so in the future. So among intellectuals and particularly in the universities, which are of course the first units of society that intellectuals impact, there has understandably been a major reaction of disillusionment with modernity during the past thirty years.

Postmodernity is the generic name for the many forms that this reaction has taken, and the many alternative views to which it has led. Characteristically, these many views can all be described as follows. In place of a quasi-behaviourist ideal of a collectivist community of like-thinking, well-socialized human ants in smoothly functioning ant hills, a new ideal of freedom and fulfilment for human persons has emerged.

It assumes the technological conveniences of the anthill as a given and is not therefore socially anarchic in an explicit way. But it is wholly individualistic about moral and aesthetic values, including those of religion; it debunks other people's absolutes most resolutely, by playful or cynical negation; it treats all public disagreements as nothing more than power struggles between representatives of different subcultures, while remaining itself dogmatically relativist on all ultimate questions; and so it is culturally anarchic in a deeply disruptive way. In postmodernity the subjectivity of the individual is set in judgment over all forms of supposedly scientific and consensual objectivity; you do not have to go along with anything that others think if you do not want to, for doing your own thing your own way is the real heart of personal humanness. In this way individuality without restraints, spirituality without truth, whimsy claiming to be wisdom, desire viewing itself as vocation and masquerading as morality, benevolent tolerance of any idea that does not tell you that you are wrong and passionate hostility to any idea that does, all linked with pluralistic pragmatism as the convention for community life, have become the leading features, indeed the essence, of postmodern culture.

As a way of life it is the egghead equivalent of Mr. Bean. We note, as we survey it, that French existentialism and American hippiedom clearly contributed to its making, and we foresee that while it is going to be perfectly happy with religion—any sort of religion—as a private hobby, it will always be implacably opposed to any requiring of a particular form of religion, on the basis that this religion, whatever it be, is right for everyone. This, then, is the position to which we have to respond in discussing the substance of Christian truth.

What happens to Christianity when postmodernity prevails? A local author has recently shown us, in his book *Mansions of the Spirit* (Michael Ingham; Toronto: Anglican Book Centre, 1997). Granted, this book was not designed as a postmodern manifesto, and I do not think the word "postmodern" occurs in the text. The author's office requires him to uphold Christianity, and that is what he believes himself to be doing. But he appears as an uncritical child of his time, and what he has actually done is recast Christianity in a postmodern frame. Drawing his inspiration directly from the Hindu and theosophical outlook institutionalized in the Parliaments of World's Religions in 1893 and 1993, and in the inter-faith movements connected with them, he offers a philosophy of religion, and a typology of religions, that fits postmodernism as hand fits glove. To look at his proposal from this point of view is very instructive.

Ingham's argument proceeds as follows:

(1) The plurality of religions in this world is a fact to welcome. Most of them are true in the sense that they mediate contact with the transcendent to good effect, and thus are health-giving and humanizing though their doctrines are mutually incompatible.

(2) The historic Christian idea that Jesus Christ must be offered to all as the only Saviour for anyone in this lost world is unacceptable, even in the inclusivist form that posits the salvation through Christ of moral and religious people who never heard of him, or if they did, rejected him.

(3) The pluralism that sees all religions as centring on God and being partly right, while partly wrong in what they say about him, is also unacceptable, for it discourages commitment to any of them, and everyone should be committed to some religion or other.

(4) All religions should be seen as centring upon a mysticism whereby those called esoterics—that is, those for whom what others call facts are merely signs and symbols of God in our souls—find harmony of experience with each other across the board, while those called exoterics—that is, those who focus on facts and truths in a subject-object frame—continue wrangling about doctrinal differences from a standpoint that is ultimately invalid.

(5) Christians should continue to worship and serve Christ and tell their stories of what he has done for them without supposing that what Christ gives them is unavailable elsewhere, or that Christ is actually needed by adherents of religions other than their own.

The evident strategy of the discussion, first to last, is to get the question of universal public truth off the table. To that end our author quietly adjusts the meaning of the word "true." All religions, he says, are true in the sense of mediating real contact with what some call "God," but in the sense of declaring what is everywhere the case and stating the problem, the provision and path for everyone alike, none of them is true. This is a thoroughly postmodern ploy.

But going this way makes the book incurably problematical, for the

Christianity with which it leaves us is not the Christianity of the New Testament, and is indeed an outright denial and abolition of it. Putting the matter more sharply still, the Christ with which *Mansions of the Spirit* leaves us is not the Christ of the New Testament, the divine Saviour and Lord whom Christians trust, love and proclaim, but a figure much less than that.

In this book "Jesus" and "Christ" become what Francis Schaeffer used to call "connotation words" and what I would call "weasel words"—that is, words on whose familiar meaning and associations (semantic field, if you will) a communicator trades while actually denying them, not perhaps explicitly, but as the lawyers say, constructively. I do not accuse the author of doing this with deceptive intent; after all, there is such a thing as what psychologists call cognitive dissonance, which is a polite phrase for muddle in the mind that keeps one out of touch with reality; but I have to say, regretfully, that wittingly or not, this is what the author actually does. Let me set out the facts.

It is a fact that from the start the Christian church proclaimed Jesus of Nazareth, crucified, risen, reigning and returning, as God's Christ, the promised Messiah, the centre of world history, now from his throne imparting to his people his transforming presence and power through the pentecostal Holy Spirit. It is a fact that apostolic Christianity was not only good news about personal salvation and supernatural living in the church, the home and the body politic, but was also a philosophy of history celebrating an imperial Lord who came the first time in humility to bear away sin and would reappear in majesty to judge all humankind, as well as to bring final bliss to his born-again followers. It is a fact that Christians from the start prayed to this Jesus and in due course found words to express the initially unthinkable thought of his personal divinity within the being of God, and the personal divinity of the Holy Spirit also.

And it is a fact that the bottom line of the apostolic proclamation was that the enthroned Christ claims the allegiance of the entire human race, here and now.

The risen Lord was understood to have told his apostles: "Go and make disciples of all nations" (Mt 28:19).

Accordingly, in a world of religious pluralism at least as complex as ours, the first-century converts "turned to God from idols to serve the living and true God, and to wait for his Son from heaven, whom he raised from the dead—Jesus, who rescues us from the coming wrath" (1 Thes 1:9-10). For they were taught that they must acknowledge the exclusive, permanent, all-embracing lordship of Jesus Christ—"The crown rights of the Redeemer," to use the old phrase—and must therefore forsake all contrary modes of religious belief and practice. So it has been in the Christian mainstream for almost two thousand years, as countless martyrdoms from the first to the present century attest. And since, as the writer to the Hebrews says, "Jesus Christ is the same yesterday and today and for ever" (Heb 13:8), it must be held that the apostolic affirmation of Christ's continuing claim on everyone's submission and allegiance is still valid, and always will be. Our Lord Jesus Christ, the eternal Saviour-Judge, remains humankind's rightful and exclusive Master.

So Ingham's suggestion that all the world's great religions be seen as belonging to God's loving plan for their own cultural sphere, and as mediating the same saving grace that Christians receive through Christ, is an idea for which there is neither basis nor room. His related idea, that a legitimized plurality of religions is what God has been aiming at all along, is pure fantasy, quite contrary to the plan of history that God has actually revealed. The Christ who will never be lord of all because his Father never meant him to be is not the Christ of apostolic and Anglican faith. What we have here is a postmodern downsizing of the universal, public, divinely revealed truth about Jesus Christ. Such downsizing must always be declined.

Where, then, is our discussion leading us? To a firmer grip, I hope, on the following facts:

(1) Christian truth is reality—by which I mean it is a map, diagram, and index of reality, and as such a doorway into it, a realization of it, and a pathway through it. I am trying here to mirror the following fact. The Bible's languages, like other languages, have a vocabulary in which the primary idea of truth is of true statements—statements, that is, that correspond to what is the case and do not deceive or mislead by falsifying how things are. But they also extend that vocabulary, so that the noun "truth" also signifies the solidity, stability, reliability, and ultimacy of the reality being spoken of, as opposed to any thought of it being a fantasy that does not belong in the world of fact or an illusion that at best is no

more than a shadow of something else. The reality to which truth in this sense is ascribed is ordinarily personal in some way: God, or a godly person, or some form of expression from either. Thus, we are told that God is a God of truth and that Jesus Christ is the truth and was full of truth, and that the Paraclete is the Spirit of truth, and when we hear of God's word as truth and of the gospel of truth the there-ness of God as guarantor of all that is said is part of the meaning that the word "truth" conveys. Thus, the truth that the church proclaims in its creeds and its preaching and expresses in its worship, and that Christians assimilate in their devotion is reality in the sense that it is not just words giving factual information about Jesus, but is the means whereby Jesus himself comes to us and generates communion between us and himself. All thought about Christian truth must start here.

(2) Christian truth is revealed reality—that is, it is truth that God himself has told or shown us. The long-standing prejudice in academic circles against the idea of God revealing truth by telling us things needs to be laid aside. Two centuries of deference to Kant and Schleiermacher have spread among Protestants the assumption that God does not use human language to communicate with us, and the Bible, whatever else it is, is not God preaching and teaching in the way that the Fathers and medievals and Reformers and Puritans thought it was. But if Jesus of Nazareth, the Galilean travelling teacher, was truly God incarnate, then his ministry is proof positive that God uses human language to instruct people, for here was God actually doing it. And once this is conceded, the church's historic belief that the Holy Spirit speaks to us today in and through the Holy Scriptures raises no new problems of principle. Granted, it is all too possible to revere Scripture as the Word of God and still handle it in naive and perverse ways, and Bible-believers need the disciplines of grammatical-historical interpretation and cultural hermeneutics as much as they need the help of the Holy Spirit if they are to know what God is saying to them out of these ancient near eastern documents. But their basic attitude to the text is right, and that is the important thing.

From the way Jesus and his apostles handled what we call the Old Testament (a complex field for investigation, which yet yields very clear conclusions on all that is significant for us here) we see that the proper approach to the Bible is to receive it as God's own record and commentary, as it were, on the historical process whereby he set up the kingdom of Christ, under which Christians now live. The church receives the canonical Scriptures as it were from the hand of its Lord as the cognitive instrument of his government over his people. Though the Bible was put on paper by human writers (prophets, poets, historians, philosophers, and pastors, each doing his own thing), and from that standpoint is as human as any collection of writings could ever be, the example of Jesus and the apostles shows us that we should hear, read, mark, learn, and inwardly digest biblical teaching as God's own witness to himself and his relationship to us, given in the form of human witness to God and our relationship to him. Augustine's declaration, "What your Scripture says, you say," Aquinas' appeal to prophecy, in the sense of God putting his words in human mouths, as the theological paradigm for the whole Bible, and the seventeenth-century distinction between God as primary author of the sixty-six books and the human writers as secondary authors, are three lines of thought that seem to point along the right path here. The God who is revealed in the shaping of key historical events for his redemptive purpose is also revealed as he explains himself in and through the scriptural testimony, and it us from this source that the definitive knowledge of revealed truth must be drawn.

(3) Christian truth is rational truth. Modernity's pundits have constantly accused Christian belief of being irrational and obscurantist; but have you ever heard of James Orr? Orr was a Scottish theologian and apologist who in 1893 produced a landmark book entitled, *The Christian View of God and the World as Centring in the Incarnation.*[4] It was a landmark because it was the first attempt in English to demonstrate the internal coherence and explanatory adequacy of the historical biblical faith when confronted with the forms modernity was taking a century ago. "He who with his whole heart believes in Jesus as the Son of God," wrote Orr, "is thereby committed to much else besides … to a view of God … of man … of sin … of Redemption … of the purpose of God in creation and history … of human destiny, found only in Christianity." And his book masterfully spells out, in late nineteenth-century terms, this series of commitments, starting with the relational reality of the Trinity, the active sovereignty of the Creator, and the enigma of fallen human nature. All his discussions yield ammunition for vindicating the rationality of Christian faith today, but none more than

what he says about the human condition. Many secular thinkers still believe (often without bothering to look) that Christianity is a facile cosmic optimism that cannot assimilate today's knowledge about the nature and history of the world, and is unable to account for the actual quality of current human experience, with its tensions, tribalisms, barbarisms, brutalities, madnesses, miseries, emptiness, and despair. But this is in fact a classic case of the pot calling the kettle black. Not only is it true that neither modernity nor postmodernity can tell us why life is like this; it is also true that when, with Orr, and Pascal before him, we see that the basic dynamics of personal and communal human life are, first, sin—original sin, as Augustine called it—corrupting all natural instincts and desires by giving them some form of egocentric twist, and then, second, God's grace in Jesus Christ redeeming and restoring while a subserving providence restrains the total destruction that sin would otherwise bring about, then the realities of disordered human lived everywhere become intelligible. It was Pascal who said that while the doctrine of original sin seems an offense to reason itself, it does in fact make sense of everything else in what Desmond Morris called the human zoo. As for biblical theism, its concept of the transcendence and immanence of the everlasting triune God proves constantly able to assimilate all the knowledge of historical events, physical processes, and operations of the psyche, that modern study can yield.

The truth is that Christian beliefs only appear irrational and incoherent when they are detached from their place in the full biblical account of things and are framed instead with the supposed wisdom of anti-supernaturalist modernity, with its secular prescription for perfecting human life. The half-way houses of liberal theology, which pander to modernity and now to postmodernity by trying to keep the Christian end up in some sort of secularist frame, are in truth the crumbling ruins of a misconceived apologetic and nurturing strategy. If, with Orr and the Christian mainstream for two millennia, we remember that the believer's commitment is, and must be, to the biblical faith as a whole, and that secular knowledge is to be related to and interpreted by that faith, rather than vice versa, we shall have our answer to every form of skepticism as to whether Christian truth is rational or not.

(4) Christian truth is redemptive truth.

This point needs less discussion, for it is so familiar; my only fear is that in our preoccupations with religious pluralism we might lose sight of it. When we are in our right minds, however, we know that the teaching of the Bible overall, and of the apostles specifically, and of the Prayer Book spectacularly, is precisely a declaring of the grace of our Lord Jesus Christ, a pointing to him as the living Lord whose dying obedience secured pardon, peace, life, and hope for all who trust him, and a celebrating of this salvation as God's overwhelming free gift. We know that here Christianity stands in contrast to all other faiths in this world: they offer simply some way out of present and future misery to those who work for it, but Christ asks us, just as we are, to receive him into our lives so that he may transform and renew us in abiding love and joy. Freedom from pain and grief is not, of course, nothing, but freedom for endless ecstasies of freedom and fulfilment and delight is much more, and this is what Christ's salvation brings.

Christians know a God whose love for them led him to give his Son to die in agony to bring them to himself. They know a Saviour whose risen body bears permanent scars from his cross, who now walks with them through this world to their heavenly home. They know a Holy Spirit who renews their twisted dispositions into the likeness of Jesus' own heart of holiness and love. They know that they have passed from death into life, and will never come under condemnation, for the blood of Jesus Christ cleanses them from all sin. No other religion offers these things; only Christians know them. Casual acquaintance with religious pluralism may make us feel Christianity is not so unique after all, since there are so many other faiths alongside it; but deeper study makes the unique glory of God's gift to those who know Christ stand out all the more. We must not lose touch with the unparalleled magnificence of the grace of God in the gospel, the redemptive reality set forth in God's message to the world, which we speak of as Christian truth.

As so often, the bottom line of what I want to say to God's people is best expressed in old hymns: lyrics of praise and prayer, embodying the timeless truths of God and godliness. Here now are two, which between them contain the essential substance of what I have wanted to say about the substance of faith and the Spirit of truth, saying it to you so that you might join me now in saying it to God:

The Substance of Truth in the Present Age

O Word of God incarnate,
O Wisdom from on high,
O Truth unchanged, unchanging,
O Light of our dark sky;
We praise thee for the radiance
That from the hallowed page,
A lantern to our footsteps,
Shines on from age to age.

The church from her dear Master
Received the gift divine,
And still that light she lifteth
O'er all the earth to shine.
It is the golden casket
Where gems of truth are stored;
It is the heaven-drawn picture
Of Christ, the living Word.

O make thy church, dear Saviour,
A lamp of burnished gold
To bear before the nations
The true light, as of old.
O teach thy wandering pilgrims
By this their path to trace
Till, clouds and darkness ended,
They see thee face to face.

That was from Bishop Walshaw How, in 1867; would that all our bishops today shared his sentiments. And this, finally, is from Charles Wesley:

Come, Holy Ghost, our hearts inspire;
    Let us thine influence prove;
Source of the old prophetic fire,
    Fountain of life and love.

Come, Holy Ghost, for moved by thee
    The prophets wrote and spoke;
Unlock the truth, thyself the key,
    Unseal the sacred book.

God through himself we then shall know
    If thou within us shine
And sound, with all thy saints below,
    The depths of love divine.

Yes. Amen.

A Note on Books

For an understanding of Anglicanism that underlies this paper, see:

Paul Avis, *Anglicanism and the Christian Church* (Edinburgh: T&T Clark and Minneapolis: Fortress Press, 1989).

George Egerton, ed. *Anglican Essentials* (Toronto: Anglican Book Centre, 1995).

Alister E. McGrath, *The Renewal of Anglicanism* (Harrisburg: Morehouse, 1993).

Stephen Neill, *Anglicanism* (4th ed., Oxford: Oxford University Press, 1977).

E. Radner and G. Sumner, eds. *Reclaiming Faith: Essays on Orthodoxy in the Episcopal Church and the Baltimore Declaration* (Grand Rapids: Eerdmans, 1992).

Stephen Sykes and John Booty, eds. *The Study of Anglicanism* (London: SPCK and Minneapolis: Fortress Press, 1988).

Oliver O'Donovan, *On the Thirty-nine Articles: A Conversation with Tudor Christianity* (Exeter: Paternoster Press, 1986).

David C.K. Watson, *I Believe in the Church* (London: Hodder & Stoughton, 1978).

The postmodern local author discussed in the text is Michael Ingham, Bishop of New Westminter. For a preliminary discussion of his book, *Mansions of the Spirit* (Toronto: Anglican Book Centre, 1997), see Ron Dart and J.I. Packer, *In a Pluralist World* (Vancouver: Regent College Publishing, 1998). For perspectives on postmodernity, see:

David Dockery, ed. *The Challenge of Postmodernism: An Evangelical Engagement* (Wheaton: Bridgepoint [Victor Books], 1995).

David Harvey, *The Condition of Postmodernity* (Cambridge, MA: Blackwell, 1989).

Gene Edward Veith, Jr., *Postmodern Times* (Wheaton: Crossway, 1994).

Brian J. Walsh and J. Richard Middleton, *Truth is Stranger than it Used to Be* (Downers Grove: IVP, 1995).

Stanley Grenz, *A Primer on Postmodernism* (Grand Rapids: Eerdmans, 1996).

Endnotes

[1] The Lambeth Conference of Anglican bishops world-wide, which meet every ten years in London (England), will be in session in July and August 1998.

[2] Paul Johnson, *Intellectuals* (London: Weidenfeld and Nicolson, 1988).

[3] W. H. Auden cited from *The Oxford Dictionary of Quotations*, 3rd ed. (London: Oxford University Press, 1980) p. 20, no. 13.

[4] James Orr, *The Christian View of God and the World as Centring in the Incarnation* (Edinburgh: Andrew Elliott, 1891).

-2-

The Comfort of Truth

Michael Treschow

"For God judged it better to bring good out of evil than not to permit any evil to exist."

—St. Augustine,
Enchiridion on Faith, Hope, and Love, VIII, 27.

Before I say anything about the comfort of truth I think I ought first to say some discomforting things about the current problem of truth. This conference takes as one of its chief concerns the difficulty in this present age to speak about, much less understand, what truth is. I do not mean that we cannot recognize merely factual truth. Most of us still tend to rely on the common sense notion that a fact is a fact, with due allowance for the finitude and fallibility of the human mind. Here we are this evening of Feb. 18, 1998 in the auditorium of St. John's Church. Few of us would dispute that this is a factual truth. But higher order truths present real difficulties today. Who are we as humans? What is our nature? What is our good? What makes a good act or a good life? In such fractious issues as abortion, euthanasia, sexual preferences, and spiritual preferences the prevailing sensibility would leave things up to an individual's own inclination as to what would fulfill his or her wishes. And so if we pursue these issues by asking about the nature of the soul and what it is fitting for it, we are today virtually out of order,

31

offensive in the very assumption that the human spirit is subject to a common, universal good. Open-endedness and indeterminacy is at present the dominant mode of judgment in matters of self-knowledge.

Postmodernism essentially fragments our understanding of ourselves, and of anything else. Shards of discourse are pieced together whimsically to make a momentary and ironic statement. Where nothing is true in any permanent sense, anything can be taken as true for the moment. This is very evident in Vancouver's own television program, *The X-Files.* The show is a grab bag of anything weird, anything paranormal, anything that is not comfortingly normal. One week it is about telepathic powers, another week African voodoo powers, another week reincarnation, another week a Jewish Golem, another week Catholic saints, another week a satanic cult, another week ghosts, and so on. And always, of course, it keeps coming back to that recurring theme of aliens and alien abduction. The show's primary motto, "The Truth is out there," is ironic and ambiguous. For the truth on this program is endlessly deferred as Scully and Mulder quest through a labyrinth of cover-ups and lies. The truth that they almost always come to is that here was yet another lie. "The Truth is out there" means for one thing that it is not here, that we cannot find it. But it could also mean that the truth is not present, it is not with us, that it does not inhere in our minds or our nature. But still another meaning is that the truth is weird — it's "out there." And what is weird, according to the old poetic sense of the word, is what turns everything upside down and leads to destruction. There is no comfort in this proclamation of truth, only foreboding. The harsh irony of the motto that "The Truth is out there" is made clear in some of the show's secondary mottoes that serve to interpret the primary motto: "Lies, Deceit, and Obfuscation" and "Trust No One." *The X-Files* largely depicts a world of falsehood.

The X-Files' success is based on the impulse running through our society that finds stimulation in being shaken up and discomforted. It mocks the limited horizons of conventional science and yet is careful to cultivate an aura of scientific credibility and even plausibility. This puts the show in the mode of science fiction, which has always dreamed that virtually anything is scientifically possible. One of the chief axioms underpinning science fiction is that powers that seem magical to one culture are really only the technology of a superior culture. Under this premise that most anything is scientifically possible a show like *The X-Files* can readily mock everything actual and conventional. Nothing in the world of *The X-Files* can be counted on (except for the compelling exceptions of Mulder and Scully who are really a filter for our reception of whatever weird thing is taking place) because the unknown swims just below the surface of common awareness, and erupts forth to confound common sensibilities. The institutions of science, government, and conventional religion are only impediments to an awareness of the limitless, open-ended possibilities as to what might be.

The current fashion trend that I see among my more avant-garde students portrays this same spirit. The tattoos, the body-piercing, the ever-changing and ever-more unnatural hair colours, the dark, heavily coloured nail polish, used now even by some young men, are all features of a spirit of self-inflicted irony. A satisfaction is taken in this disquieting distortion of the human form that seeks to render it alien, as weird in that old poetic sense. What is human today is a theme that is really only to be played upon, for there is nothing basically and essentially human to know and understand. And the current play upon the human form in fashion and upon human nature in a show such as *The X-Files* is in the mode of the deadly and grotesque, for that is precisely what is weird.

This loss of a sense of truth, of a common sense as to what it is to be human, is not a recent development, but arises from the eighteenth- and nineteenth-century romantic impulse to seek the ground of the individual self in the immanent and immediate, in the irrational and emotive as against the ordered patterns of conventional institutions such as family, church, and state. The principle of the romantic movement should be understood as the individual human spirit made absolute to itself; that is, the self seeks to become its own ground, its own basis of thought and action. This effort to render the self its own absolute becomes clarified and perfected after the romantic movement in the great apostles of existential freedom, Nietzsche and the Marquis de Sade. And for us here at the end of the twentieth century it is very important to bear in mind that the philosophy of deconstruction which inaugurated this current age of postmodernism is rooted primarily in the atheistic philosophy of Friedrich Nietzsche. And it is even more important to be aware of something that has been less obvious, that the existentialism, which was so fashionable in the midst of this century and which paved the way directly to this present postmodern age, not only was a kind of interpretative gloss on Nietzsche but also shared in the very monstrous spirit of Sade. It is now documented that Simone de Beauvoir, the reputed intellectual power behind Jean Paul Sartre, admired Sade and regarded him as the great exponent of freedom, a freedom from all rational and moral limits.[1] Nietzsche and Sade both proclaim a freedom that recognizes no external authority but arises purely out of a self-directed will to power. The will to power has no regard for any sense of common humanity, but breaks free from all social bonds in order that the self may authenticate itself as grounded wholly in itself. This is gruesomely clear in Sade who proclaims and preaches not merely perverse delight but self-actualization in the practice of inflicting the most brutal, horrible, and disgusting suffering on others, who are inevitably weaker, inevitably women and children. We may not feel ourselves to be in the orbit of Sade's thought, but its avant-garde force is at work around us. Roland Barthes' concept of *juissance* (a self-directed cultivation of joy and pleasure) has roots in Sade. Michel Foucault took grim self-satisfaction in not restraining himself from full participation in San Francisco's gay culture as his own affliction with AIDS was taking its course. He gladly shared his own death, his own horror, in that tempestuous narcissistic world. But in terms of popular culture the cinema has a well-established and flourishing tradition of giving us a vicarious thrill in the brutal suffering inflicted on others, such as we see with considerable and horrible clarity in the films of Quentin Tarantino and John Woo.

This culture of death, as Pope John Paul II has called our age, may seem strictly antithetical to any Christian culture, but it is important to recognize that it is rather a monstrous distortion of Christian thought, and moreover that it could not have come into play without Christianity's cultural foundations. The New Testament strongly and clearly teaches that reliance on external forms and institutions cannot make us whole, cannot give us a true and genuine selfhood—a true and genuine relation with God. John the Baptist castigates the Sadducees and Pharisees when they come to hear him and warns them that their status as descendants of Abraham does not give them a right relation with God (Mt 3:7-9). In the Sermon on the Mount our Lord himself explains that our obedience to the law is only of value as it proceeds

from the heart. The external form of obedience does not have any substance before the Father who sees in secret the thoughts and intentions
of the heart. Living in sound relation with the Father is not a matter of
living according to outward standards. Keeping your hand from murder
and adultery is all well and good, but this is not what makes you sound
before God. Those who are sound before God, he says, have hearts without hatred and lust, hearts that are full of love and forgiveness even
toward their enemies. When the Lord says, "Be ye therefore perfect, even
as your Father in heaven is perfect" (Mt 5:48), he is speaking of an inner
intention of goodness, an inner bearing of genuine love. He means the
same when he quotes Isaiah against the Pharisees' complaint that his disciples failed to observe ritual cleanliness: "These people honour me with
their lips, but their hearts are far from me: they worship me in vain..."
(Mk 7:6). He means the same when he quotes Hosea against the
Pharisaical reliance on good form: "I will have mercy and not sacrifice"
(Mt 12:12; Hos 6:6). He means the same when he says of the widow
and her mite, that she gave more than all the rest (Mt 12:43). And, of
course, St. Paul continues this teaching when in his epistles he explains,
picking up on an Old Testament image, that the only circumcision that
really avails is circumcision of the heart, that is an inward and spiritual
devotion of oneself to God (Rom 2:28-29; Phil 3:3; Col 2:11; Dt
10:16,30:6; Jer 4:4,32:39; Ez 11:19).

The Reformation gave heavy emphasis to this essentially biblical
idea, that to be whole we must each each ground ourselves on inwardly
apprehended truth, that is, we must each believe on Christ, each seek to
know, love, and obey Christ in our own hearts. The central message of
the Reformation is that we are not saved through our connection with
external institutional forms. The truth that sets us free must be inscribed
in our inner selves, as David puts it in his great penitential psalm: "But
lo, thou requirest truth in the inward parts, and shalt make me to understand wisdom secretly" (51:6). From the Reformation standpoint we are
substantiated with true human selfhood before God through personal,
genuine belief in Christ. (This message had been well taught throughout the Middle Ages by many church leaders; the Reformers were really
only giving it fresh emphasis.)

This principle of personal belief found renewed, revised, and still
heavier emphasis in the eighteenth-century revivals. It is noteworthy

that evangelical revivalism preceded Romanticism. Both react against rationalism. The evangelical idea that authentic belief must essentially be heartfelt in the individual is echoed in the Romantic tendency to cen-tre the self on the individual's emotional experience. Romanticism is indeed a kind of secular evangelicalism as it seeks to authenticate the self through genuine experience. When that experience is cut off from belief, cut off from participation in Christ, it does not have very far to go before it transforms into the existentialism of Nietzsche, de Beauvoir, and Sartre, wherein the individual becomes, in effect, God to him or herself with the freedom to will and to act without regard to any exter-nal pattern of nature. But such freedom leads to our land of post-modernity, whose gateway of deconstruction essentially explains human selfhood as an artificial and unstable construct. The self now has no rela-tion to a transcendent truth. It is not seen as an intellectual substance that can participate in any such truth, but must make temporary truths for itself. The self has become a kind of phantom that haunts whatever experience it may encounter or devise. The self is but a text ever in process of being written—inscribing and reinscribing itself in the shift-ing and changing thoughts and impressions of the age.

Not everyone in the present age will recognize themselves as dwelling in this land of postmodernity. Indeed many of us are still instinctively romantics. Some of the traces of goodwill in our society draw upon such instinct. For romanticism sought individual experience through a con-nectedness with something other, a primarily nature. And the connec-tion with nature has posited and continues to posit a connection with our fellow humans, with our natural species. This human connection is worked out in social relations, especially in the state. The intended openness and tolerance of our pluralistic, multicultural society arose originally from a sense of common humanity that deserved respect and fair treatment in its various cultural expressions. To be sure, this open-ness also expresses an intentional secularity that would have the state refuse any kind of identification with, or commitment to, a particular cultural, especially religious, expression. But such openness has now devolved into an absolute relativism that springs as much from radical skepticism as it does from an intentional good will to tolerate. The motto of this age can be heard in one of contemporary culture's favourite refrains: "whatever." It sums up very neatly the indifference, the listless diffidence, that underwrites our current sense of openness.

It is interesting to observe the interplay between old-style liberal Romanticism and postmodern skepticism in Bishop Ingham's book, *Mansions of the Spirit*. Much of what he says is all too old and familiar. He argues that all religions are a way to God, or at least that all respectable, institutional religions are. This position is a major concession to Eastern spirituality, but it is hardly new to the scene of Western religious discussion in the past century, as he himself notes in his frequent references to the Parliament of the World's Religions in 1893 and other developments of the Inter-Faith Movement. We hear in Ingham once again the romantic notion that the religious urgings and expressions of the human spirit are inherently valid, especially as they are institutionalized and codified in various cultural religious forms. But Ingham works out this old position with a new postmodern twist. He does not try to reconcile these world religions rationally in an old-style Western systematization. Something different is at work here, different from the mythographies of James Frazier's *Golden Bough* or Joseph Campbell's Jungian studies, which sought the common mythological base of human religion and spirituality. Ingham's theology is a "whatever" theology, that accepts radical difference and contrariety without any desire for coherence. Michael Ingham indeed appeals to some common basis of truth in all religions, in traditional Romantic mode: "All religions assert that at the heart of the universe there is one infinite uncreated reality, one Truth" (119). But in cultivating what he calls the grounded openness of a religious pluralist, someone committed to one faith but open to exploring the equally valid truth of other religions, he takes a distinctively postmodern stance. Our truth as Christians is something that is true for us, but not everyone (80, 140). We can explore the diversity of different faiths to draw upon what is true for them (125). Such eclecticism posits an irreducible diversity and calls for no consistency or coherence but rather an engagement in the deconstructionist's practice of bricolage. Ingham's use of the word truth is not straightforward, nor is it in keeping with the usual understanding of the term. He means by it, on the one hand, inaccessible mystery, and on the other hand, a communal sensibility. It evidently does not mean that which describes or is in accordance with the real.

Ingham is moving toward the approach of John Milbank, a Lecturer in Theology at Cambridge, an avowedly postmodern rising star in the Anglican theological firmament. Skepticism toward truth is his starting point (Hankey, 61). We should not seek to know the truth through intellectual understanding. "The end of modernity," he says, "means the end of a single system of truth based on universal reason, which tells us what reality is like" (Hankey, 53). Indeed his theology does not seek to gain knowledge but to articulate desire. For "desire," he says, "not Greek 'knowledge' mediates reality to us" (Hankey, 52), in that what we want gives rise to what is real. One of his conclusions then is that Christianity should allow alternatives. It should not, as he puts it, participate in the intellectual violence that restricts and stunts people's "capacity to love and conceive of the divine beauty" (Hankey, 68). Authentic Christianity, for Milbank, never excludes and never draws boundaries (Hankey, 68).

Such a position stands in contrast to historical and traditionally orthodox Christian doctrine, which has always drawn some very clear and distinct dogmatic boundaries. The Three Creeds (Art. VIII), most especially and importantly, have been a means of recognizing the specific form and character of the Christian proclamation concerning the truth about God and his relation to us. This does not mean that orthodoxy claims to have fully delimited and finally systematized the truth about God and his relation to us. Mystery is one of the most important categories of orthodox thought. "God is hid in light inaccessible," as the Apostle Paul tells us (1 Tim 6:16). What we understand about God is far from systematically defining all that God is, or is not. But we do believe that through revelation we understand something clear about God, something that is specific—and true.

When our Lord stood before Pilate he said, "for this cause came I into the world that I should bear witness unto the truth. Every one that is of the truth hears my voice" (Jn 19:37b-38a). When Pilate responded with his famous query, "What is truth?" he appears cynical, urbane, and sophisticated. It is not so much a question, after all, as it is a dismissal. For when he says this he promptly turns and leaves the Lord standing in the judgment hall. His dismissal of truth would seem wise to the present age, but in light of the gospel of John it is obdurate folly and blindness, since Christ is already known in the narrative to be truth itself. Our Lord calls himself the way and the truth and the life (Jn 14:6) and the Evangelist says of him in his prologue that "he dwelt among us...full of grace and truth" (Jn 1:14). Bishop Ingham's historicizing argument that these statements strictly and specifically apply to the historical circumstances of the early Christian community to which John was writing is not cogent (58-60, 79-80). For whatever those historical circumstances were, which is a matter of some speculation, these statements stand as universal claims all the same. The Messianic expectation of the Jews was itself international and universal in scope. St. John's intent for his record of Christ was to proclaim the Messiah, the truth for all time, the hope and desire of the nations. Everything said among men must be said in some particular historical setting. When Pythagoras explained that in right-angle triangles $a^2 + b^2 = c^2$, he did so in the sixth century B.C. on the island of Sicily in a small religious community that was devoted to discovering and living in accordance with the numerical harmony that they thought pervaded the cosmos. Pythagoras's historical setting differs markedly from ours, and it can be interesting to think about how his religious devotion informed his understanding even of his geometrical theorem. But whatever the historical peculiarities in which he developed his theorem, it still holds true for Euclidian geometry today. Bishop Ingham's position on St. John's gospel would in actuality reduce it to a sort of old, run-down heritage house—an interesting place to visit for a taste of the past, a place to see something of what things used to look like, but not really a home for us to live in now. And indeed he is sharply perceptive to this extent: John 14:6 does not offer a mansion for the spirit of the present age, unless we severely renovate it, as he seeks to do (cf. 79-80).

There is, however, no clearer instance in Christian doctrine of a *locus communis* (a common place of agreement, a mutual dwelling place, if you will, for Christian thought) than the understanding that Jesus Christ is the only-begotten Son of God. Central to this doctrine is the understanding that the fulness of God—that is the full being of God, the full glory of God, the full truth of God—dwells in him completely and uniquely. This, of course, is precisely what St. Paul says in his epistle to the Colossians, where he underlines the universal significance of Christ's being and Christ's work: "he is before all things, and by him all things consist. ... For it pleased the Father that in him should all fullness dwell; And having made peace through the blood of his cross, by him to reconcile all things unto himself; by him, I say, whether they be things in earth, or things in heaven" (Col 1:17,19-20). Jesus Christ's fullness of deity and universal redemption are inescapably central features of Christian doctrine held always, everywhere, and by everyone in history of the Christian church. To repudiate his universality is really to repudiate the Christian faith.

In the Augustinian tradition of Christian theology Christ is often referred to simply as *Veritas* (Truth). In *The City of God*, St. Augustine explained that one way to think about and understand the diversity of persons in the unity of the Trinity is to understand that the Father is being or existence in itself, the Son is Truth, and the Holy Spirit is Love. Augustine elsewhere simply calls our Lord Jesus Truth on the basis of John 14:6. His explication of this term looks to Christ as the eternal word and wisdom of God who informs and sustains all created reality and draws it back to himself by the cords of love. Calling Christ *Veritas* with this understanding in mind became a commonplace among medieval theologians from Gregory the Great in the late sixth century to John Wyclif in the late fourteenth century. Indeed John Wyclif, that great proto-Reformer, argued often and vehemently that Augustine's understanding of Christ as Truth Itself is foundational and essential to the Christian study of Scripture. For unless we understand, Wyclif argued, that the *logos*, the Word, of God is true before all time and for all time we cannot properly understand that it is true for our time. Wyclif witnessed in his own day a development vaguely comparable to what we have witnessed in ours, namely a repudiation of universal truths in favour of systems of thought called nominalism and voluntarism. These teachings taught their adherents to reject the vast metaphysical edifice of medieval Augustinian theology wherein all things were inter-related through universal truth. They instead posited the essential separateness and discreteness of all created things and the arbitrariness of their apparent relation of kind. It would be useful and salutary to look more closely at Wyclif's Christian metaphysics of truth that he sought to recover for his age, so that we could better understand and respond to our age. But we do not have time, and I doubt that at this hour we would have the urge. But what I can do, and what I believe that I should do, is broach this general metaphysics of truth in a lighter and less philosophical way, through a brief word study.

The word "truth" is a happy feature of the English language. It is, of course, one of those solid old Anglo-Saxon words that has a comforting and reassuring familiarity, even when we have not given its meaning much thought. But that is not the best thing about this word. The best thing about it is the way in which it lends itself to a scripturally-based theological reflection. For the English word "truth" closely mirrors its Hebrew semantic colleague, the word *'emeth*. Both these words refer not simply to reality or actuality but to the inherent moral bearing that sustains reality as real or actuality as actual. In English the word "truth" refers first and foremost not to what you know but to what you trust. The truth is what is trustworthy. The nature of those who are true is that they are faithful, that you can trust them. Truth refers to a constancy of nature. So the truth is not simply what we know, but what we know to be trustworthy. This is the primary, original sense of the word truth, and it still has considerable force today. It somehow rings true. The relation of the word truth to the word trust is interesting to observe. They would appear to be cognate or related words, but "trust" actually came into our language by a slightly later path. It is a loan-word, a fairly early loan-word, from Old Norse. It came to us by way of the Viking invasions, from my old ancestors. The noun "trust" (Old Norse, *traustr*) was, as is apt with the Vikings, more of a word denoting power or strength than of moral bearing. It meant "strong, firm, or secure," but also moved toward the sense of being reliable or trustworthy. In its verbal form it meant basically what we mean, to rely on or place confidence in. But the way in which this noun and verb has developed in Swedish is very instructive. The noun *tröst* has come to mean comfort, and the verb *trösta* means then to comfort or console. Here that sense of what is strong and firm has shifted towards expressing that which helps and sustains in time of need and distress, that which strengthens us when we need strength.

The logic of the Hebrew word moves on very similar semantic paths. The abstract noun *'emeth* derives from the verb *'aman*. This verb's primary meaning is "to support." From there it develops various senses, such as to stand as a pillar, to make firm and lasting or sure, to nourish or foster a child, to be reliable or trustworthy or faithful, and indeed to trust or believe. The derived abstract noun *'emeth* means firmness, faithfulness, or truth. It has a very similar semantic range as the English noun "truth." They both begin with that which is trustworthy and reliable and

41

move from there to what is known or understood.

In theological terms the Hebrew word *'emeth* has something very basic and important to teach us about the metaphysics of truth. *'emeth* is, of course, one of God's primary qualities in the Old Testament: "The truth of the Lord endureth forever" (Ps 117:2). His truth is, of course, his faithfulness, with which he abounds (Ex 34:6). But his truth is also at the same time his judgment, his instruction, his word: "thy law is truth" (Ps 119:142, as is echoed, of course, in the New Testament in our Lord's all important statement, "Thy word is truth" (Jn 17:17; cf. Dt 8:12). These two aspects of the Hebrew word *'emeth* are not separable but are one in God's nature. His unchangeable faithfulness is at once also his verity. In the Hebrew understanding of creation, his unchangeable faithfulness is the whole basis of the coherence, integrity and intelligibility of the created order. For creation is an explication of his wisdom and his word: "By the word of the Lord were the heavens made...for he spake and it was done: he commanded, and it stood fast" (Ps 33:6,9). The human soul is an especially important setting for the explication of God's truth. Being made in the image of God means that it is made to receive, conform to, and bear his word, to be in itself an explication of God's word of truth. After all, one of the key themes of the Bible deals with the human reception of and response to God's word, starting from the disobedience in the garden and proceeding right through to the end of the book of Revelation. The prophet Isaiah offers us an especially sharp moment of insight into the relation of God's truth to the human soul. Isaiah 7:9 reads in the KJV, "If ye will not believe, surely ye shall not be established." It is difficult for any translation to disclose the riches of meaning that this verse contains. The two verbal phrases in the English sentence, "will believe" and "shall be established," translate the very same verb that is used twice over in the Hebrew sentence. And that verb is *'aman*, the verb from which the noun *'emeth* derives. In Hebrew we meet just five words making up this sentence: *'im lo' ta'aminu ki lo' te'amenu*. The context of this sentence is as follows. Syria has formed a military alliance with the northern kingdom of Israel against Judah. They have marched on Jerusalem and attacked it, but have not breached it. Nevertheless King Ahaz and all the people of Judah are troubled and frightened; their hearts trembled "as the trees of the wood are moved with the wind" (7:2). But Isaiah is sent to proclaim to

Ahaz a strengthening word of prophecy against the Israelite and Syrian plan to overthrow Ahaz and set up their own puppet-king: "Thus saith the Lord, it shall not stand, neither shall it come to pass" (7:7). The Lord adds that the military might of the invader will soon be destroyed, but then further explains that to get any strength or comfort from this word, it must be believed: *im lo' ta'aminu ki lo' te'amenu,* "If ye will not believe, surely ye shall not be established." Then the Lord offers Ahaz a sign to lean on for support. And although Ahaz with a hollow and fastidious spirituality refuses to tempt the Lord by asking for a sign, a sign is given all the same. And the sign that is given is closely and mysteriously bound up with the fulfillment of word of promise, of every word of promise that God has uttered: "Behold, a virgin shall conceive and bear a son, and shall call his name Immanuel" (7:14). In the immediate context the child stands as a sign of God's enduring presence of goodness amidst his chosen people to keep them ever safe and secure from all threat of harm. For us now the sign has been manifest as the very Word of God itself. In any case, this word must be believed for it to comfort the people: *im lo' ta'aminu ki lo' te'amenu.*

This brief verse of five words, this little conditional sentence, says and means a great deal and needs considerable amplification for its force to be felt and heard. It is an invitation to rely on the Lord's word and find comfort. If you lean on the Lord's assurance, on his promise, on his word, if you take his word as your support, if you take it as the truth, as what is the most trustworthy knowledge of your life, then you will be established, you will be supported, you will be upheld by what is strong and sure and true. If you make this word your stay, you will not be moved amidst the heaving sway of the troubles that surround you. You will find comfort amidst those troubles, you will find confidence and strength. St. Augustine made much of this verse along a slightly different line. He used the Old Latin translation which was based on the Septuagint, and it reads in a very helpful way, "Unless you believe, you will not understand." From this reading of the verse St. Augustine developed his thoughts on the way in which faith seeks and finds understanding. Augustine argued that Christian faith gives the soul access to the very truth that it is made for, that it longs for and thirsts for from the depths of its being. The Hebrew does indeed suggest this elaboration on the Septuagint's reading, at least in an indirect way. For you can also amplify the Hebrew thus: to rely on the truth of the word is to gain a share of the truth in its essential stability, to begin to know the truth with certainty.

> How firm a foundation, ye saints of the Lord,
>   Is laid for your faith in his excellent Word!
> What more can he say than to you he hath said,
>   You who unto Jesus for refuge have fled?

Two important conclusions may be drawn from this verse. In the first place, it points to that stupendous scriptural truth, that God seeks to share himself with us. In the beginning he made man, male and female, in his own image and likeness. We are then made in the very core of our creaturely nature to have communion with God. As St. Augustine puts it at the beginning of the *Confessions*, God has made us for himself, and our hearts restlessly quest after him, quest to find rest and stability and peace in him. And God indeed makes himself available to us through his word. It is the ground of all creation and is inscribed therein for us to read. It is the ground of our being, the Trinity imaged in our mind, our thought, and our will. His word is, of course, revealed especially clearly and directly in Scripture, where we can hear and receive God's promises and assurances of his presence for those who will listen and obey. But we receive his word most fully and completely through belief in the Incarnate Word. For as the Word has taken on our flesh, our humanity, so the word takes up those who believe into his very divinity. Through the Incarnation believers enter into the very fulness of God's being. Such at least is the gist of St. Paul's prayer for the Ephesian Christians. He prays that from the very riches of God's glory, that is from the fullness of his being, that you "be strengthened with might by his Spirit in the inner man, that Christ may dwell in your hearts by faith; that ye, being rooted and grounded in love, may be able to comprehend with all the saints what is the breadth, and length, and height, and depth, And to know the love of Christ which passeth knowledge, that ye might be filled with all the fulness of God" (Eph 3:16b-19). Believers are given to know the fulness of his love by sharing in, by being filled with, the very substance of divine love. And thereby we are transformed into the Lord's image; we take on his nature in a new and heightened way, beyond the original inscription of his image in our creation. For by virtue of the Incarnation and the consequent gift of the Holy Spirit, we are being brought to share in God's very glory: for "we all, with open face beholding as in a glass the glory of the Lord, are changed into the same image from glory to glory, even as by the Spirit of the Lord" (2 Cor 3:18).

One important thing we then can know is that we are not alone. In company with all the saints we know God's love is fully with us. This is a great gift in the heaving sea of this present age where the human self floats and wanders as in a weary dream. In our decentred, destabilized, fragmented, post-structuralist world who could help but feel a vague sense of total isolation and abandonment. The Danish postmodern novelist Peter Høeg clarifies sharply just what underlies that vague sense.

> Once you have realized that there is no objective external world to be found, that what you know is only a filtered and processed version, then it is a short step to the thought that, in that case, other people, too, are nothing but a processed shadow, and but a short step more to the belief that every person must somehow be shut away, isolated behind their own unreliable sensory apparatus. And then the thought springs easily to mind that man is, fundamentally, alone. That the world is made up of disconnected consciousnesses, each isolated within the illusion created by its own senses, floating in a featureless vacuum. (237-238)

The postmodern wanderer may seem to luxuriate a little in his alienation. And yet the undercurrent of despair is real, narcissistic though it be. Such solipsism is ruinous. It shears us of love, corrupting and enervating the very desire to love and be loved. It has left in its wake scores of wounded, abandoned, lovelorn victims—especially among our children. The ghastly, violent loneliness that haunts our culture is palpable. Isolation is everywhere, aided and abetted by our mesmerizing media technologies. And such loneliness, as Mother Theresa once said, is the greatest disaster for the soul.

There are so many sorrows in today's world. These sorrows are due to hunger, to dislodging, to all kinds of illnesses. I am convinced that the greatest of all sorrows is to feel alone, to feel unwanted, deprived of all affection. It consists in not having anyone, in having gotten to the point

45

of forgetting what human contact is, what human love is, what it means to be wanted, to be loved, to have a family.

In such a world of loneliness as this we have a great truth, a great comforting, strengthening, and restoring truth, that can begin to bring light to the darkness of our loneliness and our shadowy, insubstantial relations.

> Fear not, he is with thee; O be not dismayed!
>   For he is thy God, he will still give thee aid.
> He'll strengthen, help thee, and cause thee to stand,
>   Upheld by his righteous, omnipotent hand.

The second important conclusion to be drawn from our verse in Isaiah is that the comfort of truth comes to us in the midst of a sea of troubles:

> God is our hope and strength, a very present help in trouble.
>   Therefore will we not fear, though the earth be changed,
> And though the hills be carried into the midst of the sea;
>   Though the waters thereof rage and swell,
> And though the mountains shake at the tempest of the same.
>   The Lord of hosts is with us; the   God of Jacob is our
> refuge.
> (Ps 46:1-4)

It was during a military invasion that Isaiah brought Ahaz the strengthening word that God is with us. And it was the night before his crucifixion that our Lord told his disciples: "These things I have spoken unto you, that in me ye might have peace. In the world ye shall have tribulation; but be of good cheer; I have overcome the world" (Jn 16:33). And it was in the context of persecution that Paul called the Lord, "the God of all comfort; who comforteth us in all our tribulation (2 Cor 1:3-4).

We are all of us troubled in various ways. "Man is born unto trouble, as the sparks fly upward," cried Job. Indeed we today live in very troubled times. Who can tell the hidden ways that we are each of us afflicted by the consumptive, sometimes sadistic, despair that pervades our culture? And beyond that general miasma we have many in our midst who are in more concrete terms sick, bereaved, grief-struck, impoverished, addicted, abused, betrayed, persecuted. The New Testament regularly deals with giving Christians comfort in the face of persecution, that special trouble for Christians who are invited to share in their Lord's sufferings. But the comforting word of the New Testament reaches everywhere, down to the depths of the general suffering of all creatures throughout creation. And that word is quite simply the word of hope:

> … the creature [creation] itself also shall be delivered from the bondage of corruption into the glorious liberty of the children of God. For we know that the whole creation groaneth and travaileth in pain together until now. And not only they, but ourselves also, which have the first fruits of the Spirit, even we ourselves groan with in ourselves, waiting for the adoption, to wit, the redemption of our body. For we are saved by hope: but hope that is seen is not hope. (Rom 8:19, 21-24a)

The comfort of Truth is really just simply that God, in his essential almightiness and utterly consistent goodness will restore everything, will turn everything to good. In her *Divine Showings* the fourteenth-century English mystic Julian of Norwich heard this truth from the Lord with great thudding emphasis: "I may make alle thing wele, and I can make alle thyng welle, and I shalle make alle thyng wele, and I wylle make alle thing welle; and thou shalt se thy selfe that alle maner of thyng shalle be welle" (ch. 31, ll. 3-6). Such hope is our present peace. We live in the knowledge that our agonies, our sufferings, our divisions within ourselves will all pass away, and we learn then to reckon with St. Paul that the sufferings of this present time, this present age, "are not worthy to be compared with the glory which shall be revealed in us" (Rom 8:18). Julian of Norwich put a very hard twist on this thought, saying that for those who hope in Christ, who know that nothing can separate them from the love of God, "there is no payne in erth ne in no nother place that shuld trobylle us, but alle thyng shulde be to us joy and blysse."

When St. Paul and Julian tell us to count it all joy they do not mean that our troubles are of no account and of no significance or that we should simply acquiesce passively to them. Our troubles are a place rather from which we may learn to seek God with all our heart, and lean wholly on his faithfulness and trust in his love.

When through the deep waters he asks thee to go,
    The rivers of woe shall not thee overflow;
For he will be with thee, thy troubles to bless,
    And sanctify to thee thy deepest distress.

It is a little more than two-and-a-half years ago now since my son Sam was diagnosed with Duchenne's muscular dystrophy, a wasting and fatal condition. Needless to say my wife, Jill, and I entered into our deepest distress when that news struck like a huge boulder tumbling upon us. Not long after the diagnosis we went to see a family counsellor in Kelowna who specializes in dealing with terminally ill children and their families. We thought she might help us get some perspective and to find ways to restore some measure of equilibrium to our family. As she questioned us about our lives and what resources we had for dealing with this trouble, it came out that we had been going to the Anglican Church in Kelowna for several years, but had recently begun to withdraw from it, because we had not received spiritual nourishment there over those years and were in great need of such nourishment now. She then made the very bold move of suggesting that we might not find what we need in any of the churches that we were trying at that time, and would do better to begin to cultivate an Eastern spirituality of resignation. What she said was indeed compelling in its way: what a relief it would be to cease from all striving and yearning and give up all disappointment. And it has a share of truth. For we must indeed learn to be still and know that God is indeed God, to accept his will and good providence. But my instinct was also very much to fight and to groan, to demand a blessing, Jacob-like, as I wrestled with God in prayer, and to moan and groan at God. After all, we are encouraged to be spiritual moaners and groaners before God. My friend Dr. Will Johnston once told me that there is a reason for our groaning when in bodily pain: it releases endorphins. A similar logic applies to our spirit as it prayerfully groans. St. Paul says that the Holy Spirit, the comforter, groans with us, making "intercession for us with groanings which cannot be uttered" (Rom 8:26). And it is from the midst of groaning in the Spirit that we move into the full assurance of God's truth, that nothing can separate us from the love of God; there is no power so great.

The soul that on Jesus hath leaned for repose
    He will not, he will not desert to his foes;
That soul, though all hell shall endeavour to shake,
    He never will leave and will never forsake.

So we ground ourselves on the knowledge that God in his truth and love will ever remain with us and will make all things well. As Christians then we are not citizens of this present age. "Our citizenship is from above." We are pilgrims here. We do not know ourselves or understand ourselves as essentially belonging to any earthly dwelling. "Here we have no continuing city, but we seek one to come" (Heb 13:14). Christians are not to make themselves at home here in this present age. We are not to expect the spirit of this age to comfort us with any sense of belonging. And yet the spirit of the age so potently pervades our hearts and minds that we tend to find ourselves inhabiting it and inhabited by it in such a way that we all too easily understand ourselves on its terms. This is an old problem for Christians. Our Lord himself, knowing how readily we grow accustomed to the spirit of the age, teaches us to pray daily to our Father, "Thy kingdom come."

Six hundred years ago Geoffrey Chaucer wrote his "Ballad of Good Counsel" to comfort and encourage his friend Sir Philip de la Vache, who led a tumultuous and at times troubled life as an attendant to various English kings, who tended to be rather unpredictable in the late fourteenth century. What Chaucer said to his friend back then remains useful to us still as means of helping us hear that our friendship is not with the world.

That thee is sent, receyve in buxumnesse;
    The wrastling for this world axeth a fal.
Her is non hoom, her nis but wildernesse;
    Forth, pilgrim, forth! forth, beste, out of thy stal!
Know thy contree, look up, thank God of al;
    Hold the heye wey and lat thy gost thee lede,
And trouthe thee shall delivere, it is not drede.

("Balade de Bon Conseyl," 15-21)

What you've been sent, receive with humble gladness.
    Wrestling for this world is asking for a fall.
Here is no home, here is but wilderness.
    Forth, pilgrim, forth! Forth beast, out of your stall!
Know your country! Look up! Thank God for all.
    Take the high road, and let your spirit steer,
And truth shall deliver you, have no fear.

Chaucer, playing on the last name of his friend (which sounds as though it means "of the Cow" in French), calls him a beast whose true pasturage is above. "Know your country," he says. Chaucer comforts his friend by confirming to him that life on earth is indeed, a howling wilderness, a wretched business, that it is, as Augustine says in the *Confessions*, a misery. How is that a comforting word? Well, it is a comfort to learn that one does not belong to this wretched business, that one does not have to accept its terms as the truth about one's life. Where you find yourself now, Chaucer tells Philip, is treacherous. But take comfort, it is not your country. It is not your home. You truly belong elsewhere. Bind yourself to Truth here and Truth will bring you there. Truth will deliver you there, Truth will bring you to the place where it will set you truly free.

One last word. Truth himself called those whose reward is in heaven, those who had renounced the friendship of the world, the salt of the earth and the light of the world (Mt 5:11-14). In our hope for our high pasturage, we do not desert the world—we benefit it. For as we let our light so shine before men we present "the God of all comfort; who comforteth us in all our tribulation that we may be able to comfort them which are in any trouble, by the comfort wherewith we ourselves are comforted by God. For as the sufferings of Christ abound in us, so our consolation aboundeth by Christ" (2 Cor 1:3-5).

In the time of the prophet Jeremiah, the city of Jerusalem was, as you know, sacked and the temple destroyed. The promise that Ahaz had heard through Isaiah, that the city would not be taken, did not apply one hundred and fifty years later. But Jeremiah prophesied a new and greater promise still. This desolation was not the end of the story; it was yet another moment for the Lord's word to give hope. Through the prophet the Lord says to this city of Jerusalem, full as it is of corpses and crushed houses, full as it is of people shattered by the Lord's wrath, "Behold I will bring it health and cure, and I will reveal unto them the abundance of peace and truth" (Jer 33:5-6). That promise applies to us now in our present exile from the heavenly Jerusalem. It must have been very distressing to have been a Jewish exile in Babylon and to have heard about the destruction of Jerusalem and of the temple, with the immediate feeling that there was nothing to go back to and that the nation was finished. Jeremiah's prophecy of abundance surely offered some consolation. But so too the letter that he had earlier sent to the exiles in Babylon must have suddenly seemed all the more to the point with the news of Jerusalem's destruction. They needed Babylon now. They needed to share in its peace. They needed to share in giving it peace. "Thus says the Lord to all the exiles who were brought from Jerusalem to Babylon…Seek the peace of the city into which I have made you go in exile, and pray for it to the Lord, because in its peace there will be peace for you" (Jer 29:4,7).

In *The City of God*, a great work of consolation and comfort, St. Augustine, though his main focus is on the hope of heaven, gives considerable emphasis to the idea that the Church has been a means of bringing peace and justice to the nations. Those who have the hope of heaven establish as they can and where they can the peace and comfort, the stability and strength, that the word of truth offers now to their age, even to this present age.

Works Cited

Hankey, Wayne J. "ReChristianizing Augustine Postmodern Style" *Animus 2* <http://www.mun.ca/animus/1997vol2/hankey1.htm> (Feb.3, 1998).

Høeg, Peter. *Borderliners*. Tr. Barbara Haveland. (New York: Farrar and Strauss and Giroux, 1994).

Ingham, Michael. *Mansions of the Spirit: The Gospel in a Multi-Faith World* (Toronto: Anglican Book Centre, 1997).

Mother Teresa. "Judgement of Love" <http://www.aracnet.com/~cfpw/Latest.htm>(Feb. 3, 1998).

Shattuck, Roger. *Forbidden Knowledge: From Prometheus to Pornography* (St. Martin's Press, 1996).

Endnotes

[1] Cf. Simone de Beauvoir, "Must We Burn Sade?" *The Marquis de Sade: an Essay* by Simone de Beauvoir, tr. Annette Michelson (New York: Grove Press, 1953). For an extensive discussion of Sade's corrupting influence on contemporary society see, Roger Shattuck, *Forbidden Knowledge: From Prometheus to Pornography* (St. Martin's Press, 1996).

-3-

Truth and Fiction
in the Present Age

Barbara Pell

To begin with, let me say that I am neither a philosopher nor a theologian but an English professor. Therefore I approach the topic of
postmodernism both personally and professionally/pragmatically. On
the one hand, there have been some disturbing developments in my discipline that have been very difficult and threatening in terms of scholar-
ship and pedagogy. On the other hand, without these tremendous
changes in some cultural conceptions of "truth" over the last decade, I
might not be standing before you as a female professor engaged in the
study of a so-called post-colonial literature. It wasn't that long ago that
the chairman of my graduate department told me that 1) women were
too flighty to do doctoral programs and 2) if I were any good I would
be studying "real" English literature not that Canadian garbage.

Therefore, while my instinctive reaction (like that of many Christian
critics) to postmodernism in literary theory and criticism is to retreat
back to the "good old days" of New Criticism and the "Great Books"
canon, it is simply not possible to turn back the clock. We must understand and respond with a Christian mind to contemporary theory and
contemporary literature.

Therefore I want briefly to address three interrelated topics in postmodernism: 1) philosophical worldview; 2) literary theory and, 3), contemporary fiction.

1. In the area of philosophy I am indebted to a book which is generally accepted to be the most lucid and accessible introduction to a Christian worldview on postmodernism: Richard Middleton and Brian Walsh's *Truth is Stranger Than It Used to Be: Biblical Faith in a Postmodern Age* (InterVarsity, 1995).

Middleton and Walsh approach postmodernism under the two most commonly used categories: the social construction of reality and of the self; and the incredulity toward metanarratives.

First, with respect to the social construction of reality and the self, they repeat the joke used many times now to explicate the three basic epistemological positions: Walter Truett Anderson tells of three umpires having a beer after a baseball game. One says, "There's balls and there's strikes and I call 'em the way they are." Another responds, "There's balls and there's strikes and I call 'em the way I see 'em." The third says, "There's balls and there's strikes, and they ain't nothin' until I call 'em" (Middleton and Walsh, 31).

The epistemological question is this: is there really a reality separate from ourselves (ump #1) or is reality simply a subjective and social human construct (ump #3)? The former position, that objective reality is perceived by the self-constructed and self-centred ego, may appeal to us as "natural," "essential," "universal," and therefore Christian. However, it is actually a product of the last 300 to 500 years of western intellectual history, depending on whether you date "modernism" from the Renaissance or from the Enlightenment. In other words, it is not automatically a Christian worldview (although we may have uncritically adopted it) but is the product of increasingly secular and humanist concepts of human autonomy, human rationality, and human historical progress—the so-called "Enlightenment project" of Western modernity.

In radical contrast, the third umpire represents the "deconstructionist" element of postmodernity. It dismantles our concept of realism based on a "metaphysics of presence" and claims that what we assume to be "present" as a given reality, and therefore directly "representable" in our description of it, is really "absent" or, to be precise, only present in "traces" of its absence. It further claims that "reality" as well as "the self" are only "constructed" by human discourse.

The "deconstructionist" position is seen by many traditionalists as stupid and irresponsible, and, as we shall see, in its ultimate manifestations it is a relativistic and nihilistic dead end. But even though it does-n't have all the answers, it does ask some very important questions of great significance for Christians who are committed to humility before the Lord of Truth and to justice before the Lord of Life. Modernism depended on a totalizing version of reality which privileged androcentric and Eurocentric power and marginalized or silenced all other experiences as inferior or "eccentric." The version of Truth that many Christians nostalgically and uncritically embrace is not Christian—it is sexist, racist, and profoundly unjust.

Secondly, Middleton and Walsh quote Jean-François Lyotard, the author of the most frequently-repeated definition of postmodernism: "Simplifying in the extreme, I define postmodernism as incredulity toward metanarratives." Metanarratives are master stories that explain, ground and legitimate the beliefs and practices of a society. The post-modern criticism of metanarratives is that they "privilege unity, homogeneity, and closure over difference, heterogeneity, otherness and openness," and therefore that certain groups of people are always excluded from these master stories, and that unjust treatment of those people is sanctioned by these stories.

For Christians the supreme metanarrative is the Bible, and postmodernism is profoundly skeptical of its truth and relevance. As I will indicate shortly, no orthodox Christian philosopher can accept the total deconstruction of the biblical metanarrative as a basis for contemporary Christian belief. Nevertheless, the intellectual arrogance of Western modernism has induced certain groups, including those who claim to be Christian, to wield their metanarratives as weapons to exclude, oppress, and silence other groups under the rubric of orthodoxy.

Postmodernism is scary—it interrogates all of our "universalized," "essentialized," "naturalized" concepts about reality, the self, and truth. But it can also be viewed positively as clearing the ground of centuries of false "metanarratives" that masqueraded as Divine Truth but were really only propaganda for legitimating exclusive hegemonies and exploitative tyrannies (usually white, Western, male, and capitalistic). Modernism was premised, not on Christian humility before Divine Truth, but on self-centred human autonomy and confidence that "mankind" could master both Truth and Creation. Such are the myths of naïve realism, liberal humanism, and scientific rationalism, and they are false gods that deserve to be destroyed.

And yet, while postmodernism has posed some challenging questions for modernism, it ultimately offers few answers for the postmodern Christian. Having deconstructed realism, postmodernism is left with no reality but infinite indeterminacy and radical undecidability. Having decentred the self, it is left with individuals who are merely the constructed products of society and language. Having demythologized all metanarratives, it is left with no standards of normativity to guide human ethics and actions. Pluralistic, carnivalistic, relativistic—no reality, no humanity, no normativity—it is no wonder that Christians reject postmodernism as the answer in their search for a contemporary worldview.

Nevertheless, in formulating a Christian worldview for the twenty-first century, I believe we must resist the temptation to retreat from postmodernism into a simple, nostalgic embrace of "the good old days" of so-called Truth, especially when it seems clear that the last five centuries of Western intellectual thought have been marked with so much human manipulation of that Truth. What good, for example, is "the faith of our fathers" if it is defined in such a way to exclude our mothers?

Here I would refer you to the second half of Middleton and Walsh's study in which they define "biblical faith in a postmodern age." Arguing that the biblical metanarrative is absolute and inclusive but not totalizing and marginalizing, they assert that "the story the Scriptures tell [answers the worldview questions about evil and redemption], contains the resources to shatter totalizing readings, to convert the reader, and to align us with God's purposes of shalom, compassion and justice"(107). Their exegesis of the Old and New Testament stories gives us a concept of human identity in "the image of God," redeemed and called to responsibility for a reality that is the Creation of a loving God. I have not done justice to their lengthy and complex argument, but merely indicated that there are Christian answers beyond postmodernism to questions about reality, the self, and the meaning and purpose of life. Those answers are predicated on scriptural truth, but they also recognize that, for now, we see through a glass darkly. Then we will see face to face (1 Cor 13:12). For Christians, perhaps, the second umpire is the most correct ("there's balls and there's strikes and I call them the way I see them"). This is the kind of epistemological position that the Anglican evangelical New Testament scholar N. T. Wright calls "critical realism" (Middleton and Walsh, 167).

2. Now I want to try to apply some of the above considerations to the field of literary theory. As I mentioned earlier, the developments in my discipline have led to a disturbing situation that has tended to threaten and marginalize traditional Christian critics. Leland Ryken, one of the most prestigious of these critics in North America says of "the landscape of current literary theory":

> Literary critics no longer speak a common language, nor is there any clear consensus about what critics should do with works of literature. This radical pluralism has produced a chaotic and bewildering situation in which undergraduate students cannot possibly grasp what is going on behind the scenes, in which young scholars find it difficult to know what direction to take, and in which older scholars undertake their work with the feeling that their approach to literature is hopelessly obsolete…. [M]any leading critical theorists and analysts of literary texts have cultivated a specialized technical vocabulary that isolates their discourse from all but a handful of trained literary scholars interested in the same critical approach (Walhout and Ryken, 294).

Peter Barry in an excellent introduction to literary and cultural theory titled *Beginning Theory* (Manchester, 1995) describes the current critical climate as a reaction to traditional ways of viewing life and literature now given the label of "liberal humanism." Like the tenets of modernism, this literary worldview will have an immediate appeal and apparent validity for many traditional Christian critics for the following reasons (as paraphrased from Barry below):

1. Good literature is of timeless significance and transcends the age in which it was written.

2. The literary text contains its own meaning within itself and doesn't require a social, historical or personal context.

3. The text must be separated from these contexts and studied in isolation "as it really is," to quote Matthew Arnold.

4. Human nature is essentially unchanging.

5. Individuality is possessed by each of us as our unique "essence" and it transcends our environmental influences.

6. The purpose of literature is essentially to enhance life and to propagate human values, but it must not be too didactic.

7. Form and content in literature must be fused in an organic way.

8. Form applies above all to the "sincerity" of the work that resides within the language of literature and that isn't judged by comparisons with (for example) external historical evidence.

9. The notion of "show don't tell" means that ideas are worthless in literature until given concrete embodiment.

10. The job of criticism is to interpret the text, and to mediate between the text and the reader. A theoretical account of the nature of literature or of reading is not useful and will distort the text (Barry, 16-21).

These marks of "liberal humanism," I must admit, I have implicitly and explicitly conveyed over the years whenever I have taught the hallmark course of any English Department: the Major Authors course. Such courses used to include Chaucer, Spenser, Shakespeare, Milton, Wordsworth, Tennyson, Hardy, Joyce, T. S. Eliot—and usually Jane Austen and possibly Virginia Woolf. (Only two women in six hundred years of literature; it should give one pause.)

In the last four decades a series of waves of critical theory have overwhelmed the liberal humanist consensus which had been established in England and North America between the 1930s and 1950s as the only possible way to read and teach literature. In the 1960s came Marxist, feminist, and psychoanalytic criticism; in the 1970s, structuralism and post-structuralism; in the 1980s, New Historicism; and in the 1990s a fragmentation that dismantles all "grand narratives" of theory and results in postcolonialism and gender studies. All these theories are characterized by an eclecticism that resists generalization but Barry outlines five underlying beliefs that mark "contemporary theory" generally (paraphrased below):

1. Many of the traditional "givens" of our existence (e.g., our gender identity, selfhood, and concept of literature) are, in fact, fluid, unstable "social constructs." In anti-essentialist terms they are "contingent" not absolute.

2. All criticism is largely determined by prior ideological commitment. Objectivity is impossible. Relativism is inevitable.

3. Language itself conditions and in fact constructs the reality we

experience. Therefore, the meaning of a text is jointly constructed by the writer and the reader.

4. Any claim to offer a definitive reading of a text is futile for the meanings in the text are always shifting, multi-faceted and ambiguous. The author furthermore is not an authority to which we can appeal.

5. All totalizing concepts (the canon of great books, the concept of transcendent human nature) are to be distrusted as simply universalized, essentialized manifestations of an androcentric, Eurocentric worldview.

Therefore in summary, postmodern literary theory teaches that:

Politics is pervasive
Language is constitutive
Meaning is contingent
Human Nature is a myth
and Truth is provisional. (Barry 34-36)

Now, our reaction to this list, especially the concept of provisional rather than absolute or objective truth in a text, may be instinctively negative. Mine certainly was until I started teaching "Literary Theory from Plato to Postmodernism" ten years ago. Then I discovered that, in terms of literary criticism, the principles I thought had been given by God were in fact formulated by the Neo-classicists, the Romantics, Matthew Arnold, and the so-called New Critics that dominated all university (and therefore high school) teaching of literature in North America after World War I. These literary critics were not speaking from a Christian worldview—in fact most of them saw literature as a replacement for a demythologized and discredited Christianity.

If one goes back before the eighteenth- century Enlightenment to a profoundly Christian Renaissance critic such as Sir Philip Sidney, one discovers that many of the literary principles we take for granted are, in fact, the product of a later secular humanism. Sidney's ideal literary text is a didactic "sugar-coated pill" that is the product of a commitment to Christianity. The author deliberately transcends his fallen human nature (infected will) and relies upon divine inspiration (erected wit) to depict a world not "realistic" or "mimetic" but idealized. And his rhetorical (that is, manipulative) use of language is judged by how well or poorly the reader incorporates the text into his/her own changed and reformed life. This theory is not exactly postmodern, but it is not New Criticism either.

Moreover, if we return to Barry's principles without prejudice, we need to admit that many of them are true. In our experience, literary texts—and here I deliberately do not include the Bible which is not a product of merely human inspiration or creation—are cultural products, invested with ideologies, communicated in language, multi-faceted in meaning, limited in truth, and often discriminatory in terms of gender and race.

I hope that I have made the parallels clear between my first section, in which I suggested that the instinctive Christian prejudice against postmodernism is partly based on Enlightenment and not on Christian philosophies, and my present section, in which I suggest that the traditional critical rejection of postmodern theories is largely based on New Criticism and not on Christian theories of literature. To continue the parallel, if postmodern theory has legitimately interrogated some of our false assumptions about literature, does it offer any answers for our reading and teaching of literary texts?

Here I would like to recommend the text that I use as a Christian companion to my Literary Theory course: Clarence Walhout and Leland Ryken eds., *Contemporary Literary Theory: A Christian Appraisal.* (Eerdmans, 1991). The literary theory most closely identified with postmodernism was first formulated by the French philosopher Jacques Derrida. It is called poststructuralism or deconstruction. Defining poststructuralism in simple language is a contradiction in terms because language, for the deconstructionist, is self-contradictory and without determinate meaning. De-constructionist philosophy, as the name would suggest, followed and opposed structuralism for being anti-humanist in claiming that the meaning of a text is not an inherent "essence," or the product of a self-conscious author's concept of the truth about human life, but simply an arbitrary product of social constructions and language codes. In 1966 Derrida "deconstructed" structuralism by pointing out its inherent contradictions in the theory and went on to dismantle the whole of the literary world.

In short, Derrida (following the philosophies of Friedrich Nietzsche and Martin Heidegger) theorized that there is nothing outside of a text which can grant it absolute or determinate meaning, i.e., that there is nothing beyond the sequence of verbal signs that it "really" refers to; not the "real world"; not the intention of the author; and not any predetermined meanings for language based on theology or the Platonic Ideal that guarantees the validity of words to convey meanings. In philosophic terms, Derrida attacks all of Western culture as naïvely "logocentric," that is, as relying on false assumptions of a "metaphysics of presence" or "transcendental signified" that grounds human communication. Having "decentred" all language Derrida reduces it to an endless "free-play" of *différence*—which is to say that words have no meaning in themselves but only refer to other words (difference) in an endless chain (deferred) of "signifiers" that can never come to rest in a final "signified" or meaning.

Of course, a text may appear to "mean" something, but that is where deconstruction can demonstrate that it has no decidable meaning, not even a finite set of possible meanings, but only an infinite range of self-contradictory indeterminacies. Where a New Critic exercises great effort and ingenuity in attempting to determine the precise meaning of a literary work and to show how all of its elements are unified and significant, the deconstructionist does the opposite. He/she unravels the text to demonstrate its contradictions, inconsistencies, absences, and multiplicities that prevent a clear unified interpretation. Or, as the most famous American deconstructionist, J. Hillis Miller, put it: "All reading is misreading."

My students' reaction to this practice of textual annihilation is usually "why would anyone—and especially English professors who make their living out of teaching literature—go to all this trouble to demonstrate that everything they have spent their careers doing is meaningless?" It is a very good question, but deconstruction has been a disturbingly powerful force in our discipline over the last two decades nevertheless and, lest you think this is all a rather esoteric academic argument, it has decisively changed the way literature is taught in our universities and high schools.

At this point radical deconstruction has mostly self-destructed on the basis of its own inconsistencies and contradictions, as John Ellis prophesied in *Against Deconstruction* (1989). As the Christian critic Alan Jacobs noted, it was ultimately "no more than the application of

Nietzschean existentialism—with its cult of power deriving from the recognition of utter autonomy—to language." Therefore, "insofar as deconstruction involves the exertion of power over texts, writers, and other interpreters. . . the Christian can join with the Marxist, [the feminist], and the liberal humanist to denounce it as ethically reprehensible" (Walhout and Ryken 193-94).

To return to the question I posed earlier—Does postmodern literary theory have any answers for a Christian reading and teaching literature?—I believe the answer is no, not in terms of deconstruction. But what about post-poststructuralism? Deconstruc-tion (as a postmodern philosophy) challenged and subverted the foundational assumptions of Western civilization and revealed that many of its assumptions were predicated on hierarchical relations that privileged certain groups (for example, European patriarchal culture) over others. Poststructuralism thus cleared the ground for the rise of other postmodern literary theories more compatible with a Christian worldview in terms of their appeal to truth and justice. Marxism, Feminism, New Historicism, Reader-Response, and Postcolonialism all variously ground their theories in ethical considerations and condemn deconstruction for its unrealistic and irresponsible treatment of both texts and history. As the critics in Walhout and Ryken's anthology point out, Christians must be very careful not to jump on the bandwagons of these contemporary literary theories without discerning the key differences between secular and Christian perspectives; but we can share their concern for social justice while predicating ours on a higher Truth. Walhout says of Marxist criticism, for example:

> Marxist critics will examine the history of literature to understand how writers have responded to the social and economic conditions of cultural life. Christian critics will examine the history of literature to understand how writers have responded both to the social conditions of life and to the reality of a divine being who transcends the material world. (91-92)

In Walhout and Ryken, Susan Gallagher says of feminism:

> With its ethical commitment and its emphasis on the influence of belief on criticism, feminist literary criticism has important similarities to the kind of criticism that Christian scholars produce.

The various ethical dimensions of feminist literary criticism may provide some models of ways to apply religious beliefs while reading literature. (247)

John Cox says of New Historicism:

In short, New Historicism enables us to perceive the cultural embeddedness of both historic art and historic criticism: that is its principal gift to the current critical scene.... If Lewis was on the edge of New Historicism in 1936, he nonetheless avoided its problems because of his rich sense of the moral order outside a historicist construction. (268)

And Michael VanderWeele says of Reader-Response:

Reader-response theory does not aim for uniformity of interpretation, nor does it assume that uniformity is possible; it does, however, help to account for the diversity of interpretations and to encourage participation in a community of interpreters. Such a goal is a worthy one for Christians, who wish to stand both within their own traditions and within culture at large. (146)

Finally, while postmodern literary theories may not authorize, as Christians do, only one version of ultimate Truth, nevertheless, they do validate "interpretative communities," among which Christian critics may legitimately claim a presence. They also encourage interdisciplinary textuality in which Christians may bring theology to bear on literature. In a personal example, next fall Wilfred Laurier University Press will publish my book, *Faith and Fiction: A Theological Critique of the Narrative Strategies of Hugh MacLennan and Morley Callaghan.* While in many ways my book is a very traditional critical text, its combination of religion and literature, and its consideration of texts not simply as aesthetic autonomies but as ideological constructs, would have been very difficult to have published in "the good old days."

So far I have briefly discussed two parallel theses:

1. Christians may instinctively reject postmodern philosophies, though not on biblical principles but on rationalist, humanist grounds. In fact, postmodernism, clears the ground of Enlightenment distortions and paves the way for a scriptural worldview of justification and sanctification.

2. Similarly, Christian literary critics may instinctively reject post-modern theories of language and literature, though not because of a Christian view of literature but because of an aesthetic theory of literary autonomy inherited from New Criticism. Yet, poststructuralism may be seen as a sensible and salutary corrective that has opened the way for a range of more ethical and ideological interpretations of literature, including a Christian theological criticism.

My third and final section proposes another parallel thesis more closely focussed on my particular field: contemporary Canadian fiction.

3. Although Christian readers may instinctively reject postmodern literature because it portrays a secular, relativistic world, this reaction is sometimes more a product of religious complacency than of scriptural sensitivity. Contemporary literature depicts the world that we are "in" even if not "of" (as Jesus prayed), and we must try to know that world in its strengths as well as its weaknesses if we are to evangelize and minister to it.

Postmodernism in literature is both a continuation of, and a reaction against, modernism—a period which is defined in literary studies as the era between World War I and World War II. "High Modernism," as exemplified in such works as T. S. Eliot's *The Wasteland*, James Joyce's *Ulysses*, and Virginia Woolf's *To the Lighthouse*, deliberately portrayed what Eliot called "the immense panorama of futility and anarchy which is contemporary history" and contrast it with the lost stability and order based on traditional concepts of society, morality, humanity, and religion. Still, within the fragmentation and dislocation of modern culture, modernism displays a nostalgia for the eternal and immutable and a confidence in the order and truth of art. Although the world may be known and portrayed only in small, subjective pieces, it is still single and knowable. Again, this is a literature which Christians may sometimes uncritically prefer to postmodernism because it presents the illusion of stable reality and the religion of "high art." But it does not really depict a Christian worldview—it is, by definition, a post-Christian aesthetic.

Postmodern literature refers to non-traditional literature since World War II and especially since 1960. Like postmodern philosophy, it rejects realism, essentialism, universalism, and metanarratives. Borrowing from a number of sources, including Jeremy Hawthorn's *A Concise Glossary of Contemporary Literary Theory* and Linda Hutcheon's *The Canadian*

Postmodern, we might define literary postmodernism with some Canadian examples.

Postmodernism rejects a transparent "representation of reality" in favour of self-reflexive, self-referential art that self-consciously foregrounds its artificiality and "social constructedness" rather than pretending to represent real life. While traditional realist literature sought to be a window to reality, postmodern literature draws attention to itself as the writing on that window. Its use of intertextuality (references to, and parodies of, past literary works) signals its awareness that literature is made not from life but from other literature. This self-reflexivity (the "artfulness" of art) could also apply to modernist literature with its belief in the autonomy and "truth" of the art object. The difference with postmodernism, according to Hutcheon, is that "this self-consciousness of art as art is paradoxically made the means to a new engagement with the social and historical world" (1). In other words, we have returned to my repeated theme that postmodernism can be seen positively as a subversion of liberal humanism in order to enable an ethical and even a scriptural and spiritual response to creation.

There are a number of interrelated characteristics of postmodernism that follow from its subversion of literary realism and truth. I will highlight three:

First by challenging cultural "universals" and the literary "centre," postmodernism gives voice and power to the previously silenced and marginalized, i.e., to postcolonial literatures (for example, Canadian), and within these literatures to regional voices (David Adams Richards in the Maritimes and Jack Hodgins on Vancouver Island), to women (Margaret Atwood, Alice Munro) to aboriginal writers (Lee Maracle, Tom King) and, I would argue, also to Christians (such as Rudy Wiebe as we shall see).

Secondly, along with the privileging of "other" voices comes the possibility of "other" forms which dismantle the traditional concepts of fixed, closed literary constructs. What were seen to be "natural" and organic expressions of coherent plot structure, motivated characterization, and transparent language are now subverted as ideological constructions of a humanist and elitist culture. The postmodern response has given rise to an explosion of mixed genres, (Alice Munro's linked-story-sequences-as-novels, Michael Ondaatje's autobio-graphy/fiction), to popular genres as literature (Timothy Findley's *The Telling of Lies* as detective fiction), and to the "revisioning" of mainstream genres from the margins (Margaret Atwood says she is trying to rewrite the traditionally male genres from a feminist perspective: for example, the *Bildungsroman* in *The Edible Woman*, the gothic novel in *Lady Oracle*, and the distopia in *The Handmaid's Tale*).

These forms deliberately foreground their cultural and ideological "processes" as opposed to naturalized "products." They resist closure—there are no Joycean "epiphanies" for the characters or neatly resolved endings for the plots. Postmodern fiction is not fixed, not closed, and not universal; it is contingent, open-ended, and particular.

Modernism also depicted a world of increasing fragmentation and human powerlessness, but with a deep nostalgia for past authority, a tragic grief for a fractured world, and a subjective idealism concerning the salvation of art. Eliot says of these fragments of past culture in *The Wasteland* "These fragments I have shored against my ruins." The postmodern writer, by contrast, celebrates rather than laments fragmentation as a liberation from the claustrophobic, fixed systems of belief—about class, race, gender, and, of course, about religion. But I would argue that these postmodern principles are not in themselves inimical to Christian expression, even though Christianity is often identified with past systems of oppression, and even though Christian writers are no longer guaranteed a privileged voice in our society. Let me mention Hugh Hood here—a conservative Catholic writer from Montreal who has dedicated himself to a twelve-volume series, *The New Age*, which documents more than a century of Canadian history and culture from a Christian perspective. Hood deliberately challenges the realist psychological novel with a form of Christian allegory, subverting traditional concepts of plot and character, in order to demonstrate not the fragmentation, but the unity of all time and place in the eternal mind of God.

Thirdly, postmodern literature, in order to "empower" marginalized voices and "revision" traditional forms, has had to deconstruct the social and literary myths of patriarchal and Eurocentric superiority. In other words, metanarratives have been replaced by "metafictions." Where "metanarratives" totalize and explain from a position of universal truth, "metafictions" self-reflexively foreground their subjective interpretations of history and reality, their "fictionality." These novels parody metanarratives from the perspective of those who have been marginalized and silenced by the dominant mythologies of our culture. In this way they demonstrate that the often violent and oppressive truth claims of "metanarratives" are also just "fictions" constructed by those in power to legitimate their position. As such, metafictions are a voice for ethical justice and social equality.

One common aspect of metafiction is intertextuality, in which a novel deliberately refers to and subverts a canonical text. The biblical text is often the target of such subversion, as in Timothy Findley's *Not Wanted on the Voyage* and Margaret Atwood's *The Handmaid's Tale*. Findley portrays Yahweh as a dying anachronism and Noah as a destructive, patriarchal tyrant. His revisionist narrative privileges the voices of Mrs. Noah, Mottyl (a calico cat), and a transvestite devil named Lucy (Lucifer). Ultimately, however, Findley (whose novels have been labelled "moral metafictions") is not deconstructing a Christian worldview but a perversion of Genesis that has sanctioned the subjugation of women and the rape of the environment. His final themes are compassion, self-sacrifice, and spiritual hope.

Similarly, Margaret Atwood's *The Handmaid's Tale* subverts a patriarchal hegemony based on a literal, but corrupt, literal application of Genesis 30. She also makes it clear, however, that the violent and oppressive metanarrative is a biblical perversion not the Christian creed. In fact, one of the most moving passages occurs when the protagonist seeks courage through her memory of the Lord's Prayer:

> My God. Who Art in the Kingdom of Heaven, which is within. I wish you would tell me Your Name, the real one I mean. But You will do as well as anything. I wish I knew what you were up to. But whatever it is, help me to get through it, please. Though maybe it's not Your doing; I don't believe for an instant that what's going on out there is what You meant. (214)

Although Findley and Atwood are certainly not Christian writers, Christians should perhaps be sympathetic to, and not threatened by these metafictional deconstructions of biblical intertextuality, for they do not subvert a faith which is Christ-centred and scripturally-informed. But they do reveal to us the profound ethical questions and moral concerns of a postmodern secular world that has not been able to find its answers in Western culture's institutionalized versions of Christianity. As I wrote some time ago in the conclusion to an article on why Christians should read contemporary literature: "If Christ is the answer, we don't have to be afraid of the questions."

So far, I've discussed contemporary Canadian literature primarily with reference to secular writers. In the late twentieth century, Canada is no different from most other Western countries in having almost no Christian writers among its most noted authors. The novelist I mentioned previously, Hugh Hood, has a respectful but very limited audience (most of you have probably never heard of him although he has published sixteen novels and ten books of short stories, all by major publishers, and is taught on a number of university Canadian literature courses.) Margaret Laurence and Robertson Davies were to some extent "religious" in their sensibilities, but represent an earlier generation of Canadian writers, and so it is probably true that Rudy Wiebe alone ranks as the only major Canadian postmodern Christian novelist at this time, and as such, deserves our attention.

A measure of Wiebe's acceptance in mainstream Canadian literature, despite his professed and prominent Christian commitment, are his two Governor General's Awards, the latest one for his best-selling novel, *A Discovery of Strangers* (1994). Moreover, Linda Hutcheon, while omitting Hood completely from *The Canadian Postmodern: A Study of Contemporary Canadian Fiction* (1988), devotes forty-six references to Wiebe and praises him as the foremost practitioner of the genre she calls "historiographic metafiction"—fiction that is intensely and self-reflexively art, but is also grounded in [an interrogation and subversion of traditional] historical, social, and political realities [and perspectives]" (13).

Wiebe's novels subvert history as "meta or master narratives" written by the winners and construct other "metafictions" from the viewpoints of the losers. Then, rather than resolve all of the ambiguities and complexities of these multiple narratives, in typical postmodern fashion he allows his readers to make up their own minds, and accept responsibility for actively granting meaning to a text, thereby ethically constructing their own history. His Christian postmodernism is expressed in a typically Mennonite concern for social justice. Wiebe was deeply influenced by the theologian John Howard Yoder, whom he encountered at Goshen

College, Indiana. Wiebe said: "[Yoder's] best book is *The Politics of Jesus* which takes apart the social situation in which Jesus lived to prove the alternatives Jesus had and why he chose to act the way he did when he could have done other kinds of things" (quoted in *Neuman Interview*, Keith, 243). Wiebe translates what Christianity calls "The Great Commission" into the artist's responsibility to be "both critic and witness" to society through his art. But "the novel is not a systematic theology"; it is a work of art that shows "man as he is" and "what man by God's grace may become" ("The Artist as a Critic and a Witness" in Keith, 42-47).

Wiebe's radical Christian mission within a non-Christian world is expressed in his first three novels. The first, *Peace Shall Destroy Many*, portrays the tensions caused within a conservative, pacifist Mennonite community caused by the influences of the larger secular and violent world during World War II. The second, *First and Vital Candle* (1966), less successfully portrays the protagonist's struggle between his lost faith and the corruption of the faithless world.

It was his third novel, *The Blue Mountains of China* (1970), however, that established Wiebe's competence and reputation in the epic mode, which has become his fictional trademark. The novel is a brilliant "historiographic metafiction" (Hutcheon 210)—a postmodern deconstruction of historical myth on a vast scale. Like his later epics about aboriginal peoples, *The Blue Mountains of China* explores the community and spirituality of a marginalized people. It covers one hundred years of Mennonite history on four continents and traces the dispersion of Russian Mennonites to Canada, China, and Paraguay through four families, nine narrative voices, and an intricate structure crisscrossing time and space. The Mennonite pilgrimage to freedom is a metaphor for the modern, universal quest for meaning; and the novel realistically explores the relative options of Christian faith and secular materialism through a postmodern structure of many voices in dialogue and debate. The novel's conclusion, however, demonstrates the problems of imposing theological closure on fictional flux. In the final chapter, the polyphonic medley of voices changes into a univocal sermon by Wiebe's spokesperson, John Reimer. He deconstructs the isolationist Mennonite myth of the Promised Land (symbolized in the title) and substitutes a theology of social responsibility: "[Jesus] was alive, on earth to lead a revolution ... for social justice" (215).

In *The Temptation of Big Bear* (1973), *The Scorched-Wood People* (1977), and *A Discovery of Strangers* (1994), Wiebe similarly creates epic historiographic metafictions which challenge authoritative texts with oral traditions. In these novels he combines religion with his other main influence, his roots in the Canadian West, and interrogates the Eurocentric conceptions of the history of Western Canada in his portrayals of the conflicts between whites and aboriginals. He depicts Big Bear as the Cree chief who defies the European linear partitioning of the prairies with an animistic devotion to the land. The Métis "Prophet," Louis Riel, gives vision and voice to his "scorched-wood people" and is crucified by white political power and capitalistic corruption. *In A Discovery of Strangers,* the spiritual attachment of the Dene people to the land is contrasted with the ecological destruction and cultural elitism of the Englishmen in the Franklin Expedition. These historical revisions self-consciously subvert the European creeds of reason and progress with native religious revelation.

Wiebe thus interrogates the concept of transparent and transcendental realism in his "metafictional" and "metaphorical" narratives (Hutcheon, 54-55). Accepting the novel as a construction, rather than as a reflection (mimesis) of reality, Wiebe foregrounds his theological assumptions in a self-reflexive version of history. He thus avoids the modern incredulity toward the spiritual, which is perhaps the central problem for the modern religious writer, by inviting his readers themselves to mediate between the spiritual text and their own secular lives. Wiebe's post-colonial ideology of social justice and his postmodern genre of historiographic metafiction may well be the Christian answer to contemporary postmodern literature.

In itself, postmodernism is a philosophical and theological dead-end. But it may have provided, providentially, a means of deconstructing the Enlightenment hubris of secular humanism. Let us now, as Christians, go beyond postmodernism to uphold the scriptural principles of Truth, Justice and Mercy—in order to witness to our fallen world.

Works Cited

Atwood, Margaret. *The Handmaid's Tale*. Toronto: Seal, 1986.

Barry, Peter. *Beginning Theory*. Manchester: Manchester University Press, 1995.

Ellis, John. *Against Deconstruction*. Princeton, N.J.: Princeton University Press, 1989.

Findley, Timothy. *Not Wanted on the Voyage*. Markham, Ont.: Penguin, 1985.

Hawthorn, Jeremy. *A Concise Glossary of Contemporary Literary Theory* London: Edward Arnold, 1992..

Hutcheon, Linda. *The Canadian Postmodern: A Study of Contemporary Canadian Fiction*. Toronto: Oxford, 1988 .

Keith, W.J. ed. *A Voice in the Land: Essays By and About Rudy Wiebe*. Edmonton: NeWest Press, 1981.

Middleton, Richard and Brian Walsh. *Truth Is Stranger Than It Used to Be: Biblical Faith in a Postmodern Age*. Downers Grove, Ill.: InterVarsity Press, 1995.

Walhout, Clarence and Leland Ryken. *Contemporary Literary Theory: A Christian Appraisal*. Grand Rapids, Mich.: Eerdmans, 1991.

Wiebe, Rudy. *The Blue Mountains of China*. Toronto: McClelland and Stewart, 1970.

-4-

Being True in
the Present Age

Craig M. Gay

My theme is "being true in the present age" and although I want to
place the emphasis, ultimately, on "being true" in light of the
Gospel of Jesus Christ, I want to begin by reflecting about "the present
age" and the way our culture understands and values knowledge and
truth. The contemporary ethos, it seems, is not only explicitly at odds
with Gospel truth at any number of points, but discloses a fundamentally instrumental and utilitarian spirit; and it is this manipulative spirit that prevents many today from apprehending the truth of the living
God. As the Jewish philosopher Martin Buber commented in his
remarkable little book *I and Thou* (1924): "One cannot divide one's life
between an actual relationship to God and an inactual I-It relationship
to the world—praying to God in truth and utilizing the world. *Whoever
knows the world as something to be utilized knows God the same way* [my
emphasis]."[1] Buber's point was that if one knows God as something to
be "utilized," then one does not really know God at all, and he went on
to suggest that it is no accident that the present age, preoccupied as it is
with utilizing truth, is secular and atheistic; for in adopting an instrumental attitude toward truth the present age nullifies the possibility of
knowing the truth of the living God.

To appreciate just why it is that knowledge and truth are only valued
today to the extent that they can be put to use, it may help to begin by

considering the three ways that we commonly use the words, "true" and "truth": We use the terms in connection with a person's character to imply fidelity, constancy, sincerity, and honesty; i.e., to be a true friend or, as the Australians say, to be "true blue." In this connection, we note that our word *truth* evolved from the Old English word *treowth*, from which the word *betrothal* is also taken. We also use the word "truth" to affirm the reality of a thing, or its actuality as confirmed by inquiry. Along this line, the predominant method of inquiry in recent centuries has been that of modern science, and we have placed a great deal of faith in science's ability to uncover the truth of things and to discover how they really are in and of themselves. Lastly, we use the word "truth" in connection with religion where it points to the truth of God and to the larger meaning of existence.

The Scriptures assert that there is—or ought to be—a consonance between the three kinds of "truth" and that it is the third—the truth of God's being and character—that establishes and confirms the truths of created nature and the truth of our lives. Consider, for example, the following excerpts from Psalm 33:

Sing joyfully to the LORD, you righteous; it is fitting for the upright to praise him...

For the word of the LORD is right and true; he is faithful in all he does.

The LORD loves righteousness and justice; the earth is full of his unfailing love.

By the word of the LORD were the heavens made, their starry host by the breath of his mouth...

From heaven the LORD looks down and sees all mankind; from his dwelling place he watches all who live on earth—he who forms the hearts of all, who considers everything they do.

No king is saved by the size of his army; no warrior escapes by his great strength...

But the eyes of the LORD are on those who fear him, on those whose hope is in his unfailing love... (NIV)

And so it is that the Scriptures enjoin us to sing joyfully to the living God, the LORD, the creator of the heavens and the earth. He is the one who controls the destinies of all peoples. He is also the one who speaks, and whose words are right and true, entirely faithful and wholly trustworthy. And not only is the living God—the LORD—the source of all truth, but his truth is of a kind that ought to elicit joy and praise, faith, hope, and love. The truth of God is not simply information. It is not data. It cannot be reduced to a formula or integrated into a calculation. It transcends propositions. Rather the truth of the living God is qualitatively conjoined with righteousness and love. It is for this reason that our knowledge of his truth must also be bound together with righteous obedience and love. Not only do we believe, as I think Augustine once said, in order that we might understand, but we know in order that we might love. Our love, furthermore, must be ordered to God's holiness. Christianly understood, "being true" means attending to God's gracious presence in the world; it means listening to his words; and responding to him with joy in obedience.

Now, we are aware that very nearly the opposite is the case in contemporary culture. In the first place, the relation characterizing the three "truths" is not one of harmony, but of disharmony. The truths revealed by the methods of modern science, for example, have been taken to invalidate the truth of the Christian religion, and indeed of all religions. This is one of the reasons why religion is not permitted to inform contemporary public life. The truths revealed by the methods of science have also been understood in such a way as to marginalize and even invalidate the possibility of truthful character. What may on the surface appear to be the integrity of a person's character is, so we are often told today, really nothing but the reflection of environmental factors and/or of biochemical processes. Conversely (and ironically) the truth of the self—or of groups of selves—is held by many today to supersede both the truths of the natural world and the truth of religion. "Being true to oneself" and/or "self-determination" has become a kind of first principle within contemporary culture. And so although the Christian claim that "all truth is God's truth" may once have held sway within Western society and culture, the contemporary declaration is that all truth is more-or-less relative to that deliberately chosen either by the self or by one's group.

Even more significantly, contemporary culture does not pursue the knowledge of truth for the sake of love, but for the sake of control. We have sought to discover the truths of nature so that we might take control over nature. We have sought to discover the truths of the psyche so that we might take control of ourselves and our destinies. Even religious truth is today sought primarily for its instrumental value either for social control or for private self-construction. Thus while Nietzsche's celebrated assertion that the use of the word "truth" always disguises a merely human agenda is not, strictly speaking, true, it does describe our culture's attitude toward truth quite perceptively.

In the following essay, I want to explore some of the reasons why our culture exhibits such a manipulative attitude toward knowledge and truth. I also want to suggest just why it is that "self-determination" has become such a magisterial principle within contemporary culture. The reason for doing both of these things is so that we can set the Bible's teaching about truth and truthfulness off in greater relief. Perhaps if we see just how radically the scriptural evaluation of truth and truthfulness differs from that of our culture we can better grasp the cost of discipleship today.

Now, it is often suggested these days — usually under the banner of "postmodernism"—that self-determination has only become the master truth of contemporary culture because we have finally seen through the false claims of the other two kinds of truth. We saw through the false claims of religion, and particularly through the notion of revealed truth, so the postmodernity argument runs, several hundred years ago following the disastrous wars of religion that succeeded the Reformation. We subsequently shifted our allegiance to the scientific method, hoping that science would deliver a more reliable truth upon which to base our lives. But, of course, we realize now that modern science, far from disclosing universal truth, has really only served as a kind of hammer in the hands of the privileged with which they have beaten back and marginalized other groups. What we need to do now that we are postmodern, is to trust ourselves, and our groups, not to discover truth, but to *construct* those "truths" (now placed in inverted commas) that serve to make our

lives meaningful. In fact, the postmodernists assert, there is no such
thing as truth. There are only various groups of people doing the best
they can to make sense of their own circumstances in an ultimately
meaningless universe and contending against each other in a context of
material scarcity.

There is, of course, a lot to be said for the postmodernity thesis. It
does describe the repressive impact that modern scientific and technological progress have actually had upon many marginalized peoples. And
yet to forsake modernism in the name of subjectivistic self-determination seems to me to be both highly ironic and exceedingly dangerous.
For the problem with modern development is not simply that certain
privileged classes have been allowed to oppress other groups in the name
of scientific progress, but that modernity's instrumental and manipulative—and supremely subjectivist—understanding of truth made this
oppression inevitable. Taking control of the world, as C. S. Lewis once
observed, always boils down to the control of some at the expense of
others.[2] To suggest that we can redress the problems of modernism by
resorting to self-determination founded on some other—but equally
idiosyncratic—basis only exacerbates modernity's manipulative tenden-
cies and virtually guarantees further oppression.

And so the problem with the present age's estimation of truth, is not
simply that we have employed destructive tools and methods under the
banner of scientific truth, or that privileged groups have defended their
privileges by oppressing others under the standard "enlightened
progress," though both have been very real sources of pain for many
people. Rather our problem is that our entire approach to life has
become so thoroughly instrumental, manipulative, and, finally, selfish,
that we can no longer apprehend the truth of the living God. While the
heavens may well declare the glory of God, as Psalm 19 affirms, we simply cannot, as a culture, hear them because we're not listening.
Modernists, postmodernists, positivists, post-structuralists, Christians,
non-Christians, etc., I think we are probably all implicated in our age's
penchant for taking an instrumental and manipulative attitude toward
truth, for such is the attitude our culture has encouraged us to take for
several centuries. Yet we must somehow break this manipulative mental
habit if we are ever to know God in truth. This is the thesis of my pre-
sentation. Now, admittedly, this may sound like something of over-reac-

tion to the present age, but let me try to flesh out my thesis by discussing what has been called the "modern project," the way knowledge and truth have been understood within it, and the impact this conception of truth has had upon the modern—and now postmodern—imagination.

The "modern project," as modernity has been called—which began to take shape in Western Europe during the fourteenth century and which continues even now to spread around the world—was launched with the deliberate decision to forswear philosophical and theological judgment— i.e., what we might term a genuinely religious view of life—for the sake of the prosperity that was to be made possible by scientific knowledge and by technological development. The disciplined examination and manipulation of nature by means of science and technology were to reveal and establish practical truths that we could really live by; and it was hoped that science and technology would provide a surer foundation for social order and personal happiness than traditional religion had been able to do. As Sigmund Freud contended earlier this century in his famous essay on religion, "The Future of an Illusion" (1927):

> Men cannot remain children forever... Need I confess to you that the sole purpose of my book is to point out the necessity for this forward step?... By withdrawing their expectations from the other world and concentrating all their liberated energies into their life on earth, they will probably succeed in achieving a state of things in which life will become tolerable for everyone and civilization no longer oppressive to anyone.[3]

And so we have, at least since the seventeenth century and repeatedly thereafter, been encouraged to forswear religious understanding for the sake of such things as peace, prosperity, comfort and convenience.

Of course, the edge was taken off of this repudiation of a religious view of life by means of a clever reinterpretation of religion. Jean Jacques Rousseau (1712-1778), for example, contended that what had once been understood to be metaphysical sources of truth—i.e., such as Holy Scripture—were really only primitive expressions of human longing for such things as liberty and equality. Or, as Ludwig Feuerbach would put it c. 1840: "The yearning of man after something above himself is nothing else than the longing after the perfect type of his nature, the yearning to be free from himself, i.e., from the limits and defects of his individuality."[4] This inventive reinterpretation of the meaning of religion is one of the reasons why "hermeneutics"—the study of interpretation—has become such a central concern within modern, and now postmodern, intellectual discourse. It also goes some distance toward explaining how traditional religious understanding has been domesticated and put to use within modern psychology. As Philip Rieff observed in his classic study *The Triumph of the Therapeutic* (1966), in his independence from all gods, modern "psychological man" feels free to use god language and, indeed, to use any faith that lends itself to therapeutic use, but he cannot really believe anything.[5] It is this psychological reinterpretation of religion as projected human desire that has, together with the commitment to scientific and technological development, enabled ours to become one of the only truly secular cultures in human history.

And yet, as we know, many today have begun to suspect—as others have suspected all along—that the kind of truth revealed by the methods of modern science will never really be humanly satisfying. Not only has the scientific investigation into nature failed to reveal who we really are and what really makes us happy, but science's habit of "objectifying" nature—of rendering it as a manipulable thing or object—for the sake of taking control of it has left us surrounded by a whole host of impersonal and manipulative social structures and customs. Indeed, the manipulative quality of modern scientific culture is evident even in the private sphere of self-construction, for it appears that self-constructing individuals quite often envision and treat even themselves as manipulable objects. Yet instead of criticizing the manipulative attitude toward truth that lies at the heart of the modern project, recent critics of modernism have focused only upon the question of "who has been allowed to control whom," and have—ironically—advocated an even more thoroughly instrumental understanding of truth as the solution to modern problems.

At any rate, it appears that our preoccupation with control, and with knowing solely for the sake of taking control of things, explains why modern—and now postmodern—self-understanding is unwilling, and is by now largely incapable, of appreciating any meaning or significance in the world save that which has been "socially constructed." As Hannah Arendt suggested a number of years ago, today we do not understand

79

the human task in terms of "knowing" (*homo sapien*), but primarily in terms of "making" (*homo faber*).[6] Indeed, we understand ourselves as the beings who must continually construct, build, and fabricate by means of science and technology. This self-understanding naturally gives rise to a kind of restless activism in which, finally, we imagine ourselves to be the only creative agents in the universe. And so we don't really expect the world to be intrinsically meaningful today; indeed, we don't want it to be, for this would imply limits to our freedom of self-construction.

If we are to appreciate the Gospel's understanding of truth and truthfulness, then, we will need to renounce the manipulative habits of mind that have produced contemporary culture, powerful as they are and successful as they have undoubtedly been. We will also need to carefully evaluate the quality of relatedness—to God, to others, and to the world—that contemporary culture discloses. Along this line, we still stand to learn a great deal from the little book I mentioned at the outset, Martin Buber's *I and Thou* (1924).

By the time Buber wrote *I and Thou* in the 1920s, many had already observed that the impersonality of modern society and culture seemed somehow related to the growth of "objectivity" in modern science and technology, in political affairs, and in modern economic life. Buber's concern in *I and Thou* was to try to explain this correlation at the deepest level. He began by observing that the human attitude toward the world is basically two-sided. The world may be viewed as an "object," in effect, ontologically inferior to the knowing subject, in which case it will be experienced in terms of the juxtaposition of "I" and "it." Or the world may be beheld as a genuine "other," that is, on an ontological par with us as we behold it. In this latter case, the world will be experienced personally as in the relation between an "I" and a "Thou." To the extent that we desire to achieve control over the world, Buber continued, we will be attracted by the utility of rendering it "objectively," for rendering the world in terms of potentially manipulable objects is far easier and much more conducive to effective management than contemplating the world, admiring her, entering into genuine dialogue with her, and caring for her. Along this line, Buber observed that the "objectification" of the world has become, just as we have seen, a kind of hallmark of modern civilization.

Yet Buber also observed that the self-understanding emerging out of the "I-It" conjunction is fundamentally different from that which is made possible in the "I-Thou" relation, and this is the heart of his argument. The act of objectification, Buber observed, does not really require one's whole self, but rather discloses a kind of one-sided relation in which there is really only one active voice. The "I-it" conjunction does not really expose the self, therefore, to possibility of relational mutuality. It does not require nor does it foster self-transcendence. As Alister McFadyen noted recently in a study entitled The Call to Personhood (1990):

> Intending someone or something as an object is to intend the relation as a monologue. For an object is intended and perceived as having no independent meaning or existence apart from this relation. It cannot offer a point of moral resistance because it is not perceived as ethically transcendent. The relation can only be exploitative and manipulative.... The I of an I-It relation has an unbounded sense of its proper claims, seeking from the other only that which is a confirmatory repetition of itself. In seeking oneself from the other, one is engaged in a one-way communication open only to oneself....[7]

Of course, although this "one-way communication open only to oneself" may enhance our ability to control the world in certain respects, it inhibits our ability to enter into an "I-Thou," or genuinely personal, relation with the world, with other people, and ultimately with God, and so is extremely costly in human terms. In the first instance, the objective attitude essentially prevents us from apprehending such things as beauty; for anything that is appreciated only as a "resource"—that is, as something to be utilized—cannot really be apprehended as beautiful.[8] The objective spirit is also quite obviously destructive of any number of relationships that it is possible to have with other persons. For while the objective utilization of others may be of some benefit to instrumental rationality and may improve our ability to "get things done" in the world, it is not at all conducive to such things as marriage, family, friendship, and fellowship. It is not at all conducive to worship either. Indeed, the objective attitude is largely atheistic, even if only tacitly and practically so, for the possibility of truly spiritual relationality simply does not survive the process of objectification. While it is true that the various idols do not seem to mind being treated as objects, the living God does not allow himself to be known "objectively," that is, as an object of human planning and manipulation. If we seek to know him in this fashion, he quite quickly retreats from our view. As Buber noted in a collection of essays entitled *The Eclipse of God* (1952): "[I]t has become necessary to proclaim that God is 'dead.' Actually, this proclamation means only that man has become incapable of apprehending a reality absolutely independent of himself and of having a relation with it...."[9]

It is precisely our modern preoccupation with control, in other words, and with knowing solely for the sake of taking control, that has led to the widespread impression that God is distant and/or disinterested. Preoccupied with establishing mastery over nature, over our social circumstances, over others, and even over ourselves, the modern and now "postmodern" mind assumes that God must be preoccupied with the same things and in much the same way. "[T]he unbelieving marrow of the capricious man," Buber observed, "cannot perceive anything but unbelief and caprice, positing ends and devising means. His world is devoid of sacrifice and grace, encounter and presence, but shot through with ends and means."[10] And so it is that our knowledge and experience of the truth of God are quite directly related to our ability to sustain "I-Thou" relations and, indeed, to our capacity to apprehend "otherness" in general.

And so we might say that the key to "being true in the present age" lies, not simply in the assertion of biblical truth— though, of course, we must continue to proclaim the Gospel—but lies also in our recovery, as Christians, of the possibility of genuinely personal relationality. We must somehow recover our capacity for relating to the world, to others, and ultimately to God in such a way as not simply to reduce them all to objects potentially subject to our control. Such a rediscovery of truly personal relationality would pose an elementary yet profound challenge to the preoccupation with self which holds much of the modern—and now postmodern—world together.

Of course, recovering personal relationality is far more easily said than done, especially under present conditions. For we must begin by conceding that we cannot manage this recovery all by ourselves. Indeed, as the nature of personal existence is dialogical and dialectical, we need to begin by confessing that we must be invited—indeed, called—into personal relation with each other and with God by God himself, and that our response to this call—which is itself a gift of grace—must be to surrender ourselves to God and to our neighbour in love. Such a confession will not come at all naturally in the context of our culture of manipulative narcissism. Yet apart from surrendering ourselves to others—and ultimately to God in Christ—in love and trust, the only other possibility is for us to remain stuck in what McFadyen termed the "one way communication open only to oneself."

Happily, the Church exists to bear witness to the fact that we have been graciously invited into a personal relationship with the living God. Indeed, the Church exists to bear witness to the possibility of sharing eternally in the personal communion of the Father, the Son and the Holy Spirit. This is the life of the world to come over and against which the possibilities of this-worldly existence pale into insignificance and worthlessness. This is also the essence of the kingdom of God that Christians already mysteriously bear within themselves. In terms of our analysis above, the Church exists to bear witness to the possibility of experiencing God's infinitely loving and gracious Otherness, and thus to bear witness to the possibility of genuinely personal—and truthful—existence in and through him.

How does the Church bear witness to the possibility of entering into fellowship with the living God? Certainly not by mimicking the falsely "objective" spirit of the age and by trying to demonstrate the "cash value" of Christian faith with respect to those tasks that the world has set for "religion." Neither does the Church bear witness to the possibility of genuinely personal relationality by surrendering to the therapeutic sensibilities of contemporary culture which ultimately deny this possibility in their advocacy of autonomous self-construction. Both of these apologetic strategies are attractive today because they appear to demonstrate the relevance of Christian faith within contemporary culture. Indeed, both strategies are presently employed by churches of both "liberal" and "conservative" theological persuasions. But it should be amply clear by now that, to the extent that the Christian faith is made to appear attractive from the point of view of the present age, this probably means that faith has somehow been emptied of the possibility of any real encounter with the living God, and so has really ceased to be faith at all. We speak most prophetically today, then, simply by bearing witness to the possibility of knowing a *living* God. This is the relation that Christian doctrine has been designed to protect. It is also the one possibility that our secular and impersonal modern world has almost completely lost sight of, in spite of its largely Christian origins.

Prayer is perhaps the Church's single most important witness to the living God—at least so long as prayer is not itself surrendered to the therapeutic or to the logic of technique—for real prayer is a dialogue. It discloses a genuinely personal relation. Jesus has called us to pray to the Father, not because the Father does not already know what we need (Mt 6:8), but because he desires to see us enter into a living relation with the Father. He wants us to entrust ourselves to the Father on the sure basis of His completed work and by the empowering presence of the Holy Spirit. In this connection, the apostle Paul tells us that we are saved "by grace through faith" (Eph 2:8). We are saved by grace because the invitation to enter into dialogue with the living God is, and can only be, issued by God himself. The invitation, as Paul says, is "the gift of God." We are saved through faith, furthermore, because our faith indicates that we have ourselves chosen to enter into a living conversation with God. Faith moves us to read the Scriptures because we believe that the living God is speaking to us in and through them, and faith also leads us to pray because we believe that the living God answers prayer. Conversely, if we do not read, and if we do not pray, what else can this mean except, either that we do not want to converse with God, or that we have lost confidence in God's willingness —and perhaps even in his ability—to keep the conversation going?

The spiritual disciplines of waiting and watching for God need to be mentioned in connection with prayer, however, for God's answers to our prayers are rarely obvious, and his presence in the world is often ambiguous and hidden. Indeed, God's presence and work in the world is always such as to call for our interpretation. Along this line, we might say that his presence is such as to uphold belief, but it is also rather easily "explained away" by unbelief. With respect to the latter, it is precisely God's "hiddenness" and the ambiguity of his presence and work in the world that tempt many to doubt that he cares for us, and perhaps even to doubt that he exists at all. Yet it is important to stress that the kind of "proof" that unbelieving humanity demands of God's existence effectively obviates the need for faith and so denies the heart of the Gospel which is "by faith from first to last" (Rom 1:17). In fact, under modern conditions the demand for "proof" most often only discloses the attempt to objectify our relation with God and to confine him within an "I-it" conjunction. But, here again, God does not allow himself to be known in this way. While he constantly confirms and demonstrates his gracious presence to those who place their trust in him, he refuses to adhere to merely human criteria for demonstrability. As Klaus Bockmuehl observed: "Demonstrability has man as its subject; man controls what is demonstrable. But demonstration has God as its subject; it thus confirms the freedom of God and the absence of human control."[11]

From the perspective of faith, then, God's "hiddenness" and the ambiguity of his work in the world bespeak his graciousness towards us. After all, it is ultimately for our sakes and not for his own that God has chosen to reveal himself only to those who earnestly seek him (Heb 11:6), for it is only through earnest faith that we are enabled to enter into life, that is, into truly personal communion with the Father, the Son and the Holy Spirit. It is for this reason that it would be pointless—and even counterproductive—for God to reveal himself too unambiguously at present. The interests of genuine faith and trust would simply not be served in the provocation of grudging submission. Of course, Scripture does speak of a time when God will reveal himself incontrovertibly, and that, indeed, on that day *every* knee will bow before God and *every* tongue will swear by him (Isa 45:23; Rom 14: 11). Yet this unanimous confession of God's sovereign presence in the world waits for the end of history; it waits for the day of judgment, when the time for coming to faith shall have passed. At present we must wait and watch for God in faith, hope, and love. This is often difficult, but we should take heart in this necessity, for it means that there is still time to repent and to be forgiven for our sins. Besides, if we wait and watch for God, we will see him. As Christoph Blumhardt observed: "If one is watchful, one is always able to say something about the works of God. They happen all around us, in our hearts, and in our neighbors. If one is not watchful, though, one does not see anything."[12]

That the presence and work of God are disclosed only to those who wait and watch for him raises rather serious questions about the presumptive activism which characterizes the life of the contemporary

North American church. In fact, the contemporary preoccupation with such things as planning, with the organization and mobilization of resources, with "programming," with the projection of the Church's influence within the culture, etc., may actually be destructive of real faith. For not only does activism precipitate the phenomenon of ministry "burn-out," but even more significantly it diverts our attention— and that of the watching world—away from God's agency and toward our own. And so, although Christian activism is very much in step with the manipulative spirit of the present age, it appears to be profoundly out of step with the Spirit of Christ. Indeed, it would seem to be a rather sure route to practical atheism.

In addition to prayer and to the spiritual disciplines of waiting and watching for God, the quality of our actual relation to God must be demonstrated in discipleship and in obedience to his Word. Perhaps it is unnecessary even to say this, but the human condition in sin is such that knowledge is often detached from love, and our words are often disconnected from the habits of our hearts. Thus although we are surrounded by a great deal of talk about religious experience today, and even by talk about God's presence in the world, we must insist that all such talk comes to naught as a genuine witness to God's Otherness— that is, it comes to naught as a witness to the possibility of really knowing the *living* God—unless it is accompanied by holiness. After all, religious experience as such may not actually dislodge the autonomous self from its position at the center of its own universe, and the deceitfulness of the human heart is such that the failure of religious experience to "de-center" the self is not always self-evident.[13]

It is only in the ethical claims of righteousness, then, that the self encounters God's otherness in such a way as to limit its selfish desire to define itself; and it is often only in the act of submitting to the discipline of righteousness that we are given an indication that we are indeed participating in a living, two-sided conversation with God. This is why Jesus said (Jn 15:10): "If you obey my commands, you will remain in my love, just as I have obeyed my Father's commands and remain in his love." This is also why James writes that we are justified by what we do, and not by faith alone (Jas 2:24), for in the fallen context our deeds must confirm—even to ourselves!—that our faithful speech has indeed issued from a regenerate heart.

Unfortunately, many of our churches today attempt to mitigate the offense that the Gospel gives to modern sensibilities by failing to stress that faith must express itself in obedience. Instead of conveying that our lives in Christ must rest upon the foundation of repentance and holiness, the Gospel is often presented today as a kind of reflection of the depth of one's own innate spirituality. While perhaps of fleeting utility in capturing the world's attention, such a strategy only encourages the self-centered self to remain so, perhaps forever. Yet how could this possibly be construed to be good news? By evading the matter of righteousness, such a truncated "gospel" sidesteps—albeit largely unintentionally—the issue of Otherness, and effectively forecloses on the possibility of truly personal existence. This is tragic. For from what other source can the Gospel of the possibility of really knowing God and of participating in his eternal "being in communion" be expected to come if not from the Christian Church? To the extent that we fail to preach this Gospel, then, we have, especially under modern conditions, become tasteless salt that deserves only to be trampled underfoot (Mt 5:13). As James Hitchcock observed in an article entitled "Self, Jesus, and God":

> If all religious "revelation" is treated as an expression of the ongoing spiritual search either of individuals or peoples, then it holds no ultimate authority over the self, is indeed merely an emanation of that self.... But one of the purposes of authentic Christianity is to take people out of themselves, to provide them with the means to overcome self-centredness and distorted self-love.[14]

We only overcome self-centredness and distorted self-love in the obedience that comes from faith. "If you hold to my teaching," Jesus said to those who had begun to put their faith in him (Jn 8:31-32), "you are really my disciples. Then you will know the truth, and the truth will set you free." "If you love me," Jesus also said (Jn 14:15-17), "you will obey what I command. And I will ask the Father, and he will give you another Counselor to be with you forever—the Spirit of truth. The world cannot accept him, because it neither sees him nor knows him. But you know him, for he lives with you and will be in you." Now, this is genuinely good news, for we are hereby assured that we will be upheld by the gracious presence of the God the Holy Spirit, as we obey the commands of God the Son, to the glory of God the Father. It is thus ultimately by the grace of the Lord Jesus Christ, and the love of God, and the fellowship of the Holy Spirit that the Church is enabled to live in truth.

Of course, if we are not watching, we will not see this; and if we are not listening, we will not hear it. And if, in our hearts, we are not willing to obey, then we will neither watch nor listen. And so we must pray with the apostle Paul (Phil 2:13), that God will work in us both to will and to act according to his good purpose. Amen.

Craig M. Gay

Endnotes

[1] Martin Buber, *I and Thou*, translated by Walter Kaufmann (New York: Charles Scribner's Sons, 1970 [1924]): 156.

[2] C. S. Lewis, *The Abolition of Man* (Glasgow: Collins, 1984 [1943]): 35.

[3] Sigmund Freud, *The Future of an Illusion*, translated by James Strachey (New York: W. W. Norton, 1961[1927]): 49, 50.

[4] Ludwig Feuerbach, *The Essence of Christianity*, translated by George Eliot (New York: Harper & Row, 1957 [1841]): 281.

[5] Philip Rieff, *The Triumph of the Therapeutic: Uses of Faith After Freud* (London: Chatto & Windus, 1966).

[6] See Hannah Arendt, *The Human Condition* (Chicago: University of Chicago Press, 1958).

[7] Alistair I. McFadyen, *The Call the Personhood: A Christian Theory of the Individual in Social Relationships* (Cambridge: Cambridge University Press, 1990): 122-23.

[8] George Grant, *Technology and Justice* (Toronto: Anansi, 1986): 51.

[9] Martin Buber, *The Eclipse of God: Studies in the Relation Between Religion and Philosophy* (New York: Harper & Row, 1952): 14.

[10] Buber, *I and Thou*, 110.

[11] Klaus Bockmuehl, *The Unreal God of Modern Theology: Bultmann, Barth, and the Theology of Atheism, A Call to Recovering the Truth of God's Reality* (Colorado Springs: Helmers & Howard, 1988): 152.

[12] Blumhardt cited in Karl Barth, *Action in Waiting for the Kingdom of God*, trans. by the Hutterian Society of Brothers (Norfolk, CT: Deer Spring Press, 1979): 24.

[13] See, for example, Merold Westphal, "Religious Experience as Self-Transcendence and Self-Deception," in *Faith and Philosophy* 9 (April 1992): 168-93.

[14] James Hitchcock, "Self, Jesus, and God: The Roots of Religious Secularization," in *Summons to Faith and Renewal: Christian Renewal in a Post- Christian World*, ed. Peter S. Williamson & Kevin Perotta (Ann Arbor, MI: Servant, 1983): 34-5.

5

The Truth of Creation
in the Present Age

Loren Wilkinson

The phrase "the truth of creation" can mean several things. In the first half of this paper I will speak briefly of three of them. First, creation is a necessary premise of science; second, creation is the foundation for art; and third, creation is the sustainer of our physical, organic life. In different ways, each of these fundamental aspects of the truth of creation has been under attack in this century, an attack which is subtly but clearly related to our denial of the Creator.

At the same time, these truths have not been completely forgotten, and are being recovered and defended with ever greater vigour. Christians should rejoice at this: for to understand rightly the truth of creation in each of these areas—science, art, and ecology—is to recover a fourth aspect of creation which underlies all of them: that is, creation as word, message, news, about God the Creator. Creation is like a great waterfall, drenching us in God's mercy, sustaining us not just with food, air and water, but with the very gift of being. Many today make their first move toward the good news of the Gospel by responding to the good news of creation, a news which goes out to the ends of the earth. So in the second half of the paper I would like to look briefly at the work of two contemporary writers, one a novelist and one a poet, who record in very different ways the effect on them of "the truth of creation."

Before proceeding any further, it is necessary to reflect a bit on that phrase, "the truth of creation." To begin with, I am not speaking simply of the fact of creation, in the undeniable (if often overlooked) sense that we live in a world which does not have to be. In that sense "creation" is commonly used—along with words like "nature" and "universe" and "world" to describe "everything that is." We need some word to encompass the mysterious fact that "there is something rather than nothing," and in that sense "creation" is often used by people, with no other metaphysical commitments, to simply speak of the sum total of what is. Now it is obvious that science, art, and life itself depend on the fact that there is something rather than nothing. But I am arguing here for a good deal more than that tautology.

The crucial phrase is the "truth of creation," and here the matter gets more complex and more debatable. There are, in the history of philosophical reflection, two main meanings of the word "truth." Truth can mean a correspondence between something and a description of it, as when we say, perhaps of a deposition in court, that it is a "true account." Or truth can mean an interior integrity, as when we say that something runs "true to itself." This is a coherence theory of truth. More recently, particularly by Martin Heidegger and the twentieth-century movement of phenomenology, truth has been said to be "disclosedness" or "uncon-cealment." (Heidegger argues this, plausibly, on the basis of the Greek word for truth, *aletheia*, which can be translated as something like "unhiddenness.")[1] All of these notions of truth—including this more recent "phenomenological" one—speak of some some element of "meaning" or "intelligibility." They say of a state of affairs that it corresponds to something else, or that it coheres within itself, or that it shows forth what it is. But each of these descriptions implies a judgment that must be made outside the thing which is being described. Every idea of truth requires some "outside" or "other" to the thing which is said to be true—and does so in a double sense. To speak of truth not only requires reference to something other than the thing which is true; it also requires a person as well who will mean and believe the truth.

To speak of the truth of creation implies therefore, that personality is central to the universe. We are not determined by the sum total of the universe, but have a standpoint which is in some sense outside it, not determined by it; otherwise "truth" could have no meaning. The phrase "the truth of creation" thus leads us out of that minimalist meaning of creation ("everything that is") and into something much more profound: a recognition that to speak of the truth of creation is to be in some sort of relationship, acknowledged or not, with that which is its source. To speak of "the truth of creation" (or "truth" at all, for that matter) is implicitly to evoke the Creator, which is undoubtedly why "truth" today is seen by many as an outmoded, imperialistic freedom-limiting idea. Thus Michel Foucault speaks of all truths as "regimes" of truth, humanly constructed only for the purposes of achieving and maintaining power.[2]

Against this idea that "truth" is nothing more than the self-serving sum of our constructions, the truth of creation, endlessly probed by the whole scientific tradition, experienced and explored in art, and defended by environmentalists, stands in massive witness against the whole postmodern drift towards nihilism.

To sum up this necessarily dense introduction: I am not speaking simply of the fact of creation. I am arguing rather that major areas of human experience and understanding depend utterly on the assumption that creation is true: that it speaks faithfully of something beyond and other than itself, on which it depends, and that at the same time it evokes a response of belief and action in us. Let us consider three of those areas where we encounter the truth of creation.

1. The truth of creation is the premise of science

Carved over the great door of the Cavendish Laboratory at Cambridge University is the Latin text of Psalm 111: 2: "The works of the Lord are great, sought out of all them that have pleasure therein." In this century, crucial work leading both to the splitting of the atom and to the discovery and description of DNA was done at the Cavendish laboratories. The tradition of science at Cambridge which the Cavendish laboratories represent reaches back through Maxwell, Darwin and Isaac Newton. Probably no other institution has been the location for the doing of so much basic science over such a long period. To the many people who still assume a deep tension between science and Christianity, the inscription over the Cavendish doors must seem like a mere relic of a pious age. Yet it is worth noting, that when the New Cavendish laboratories were built, the same verse was inscribed over the doors of the new building.

The Truth of Creation in the Present Age

The Cavendish inscription implicitly acknowledges that science is rooted in Christian belief in a Creator. That connection has been well-argued in a number of works, most notably in R. Hooykas, *Religion and the Rise of Modern Science*[3] and Stanley Jaki's Gifford lectures of 1975 and 1976, published under the title *The Road of Science and the Ways to God*. Both point out (in far too much detail to go into here) the importance of the "two books" tradition in the origin of science. The Franciscan thinker Bonaventure put the central idea very clearly in the thirteenth century, in *The Mind's Road to God* [*Itinerarium mentis in Deum*](a title which Jaki's work seems to echo). In expounding the idea that the Creator has left "traces" or "exemplars" of himself through all of creation, Bonaventure writes, at the conclusion of a chapter titled significantly, "On the Stages of the Ascent Into God and on Contemplating Him Through His Vestiges [literally, 'Footprints']In the Universe" that:

> Whoever therefore, is not enlightened by such splendour of created things is blind; whoever is not awakened by such outcries is deaf; whoever does not praise God because of all these effects is dumb; whoever does not discover the First Principle from such clear signs is a fool. Therefore open your eyes, alert the ears of your spirit, open your lips and apply your heart, so that in all creatures you may see, hear, love and worship, glorify and honour your God....[4]

Thus to understand the works of the Lord it is necessary to read not only the book of Scripture, but the book of creation. Science was born (and to a large extent, continues) on that basis: that creation can be trusted about what it tells us about itself, because it reflects a "truth" beyond itself.

In his introduction to *The Road of Science and the Ways to God*, Jaki sums up very well this connection between science and "the truth of creation in the present age":

> Science found its only viable birth within a cultural matrix permeated by a firm conviction about the mind's ability to find in the realm of things and persons a pointer to their Creator. All great creative advances of science have been made in terms of an epistemology germane to that conviction, and whenever that episte-

mology was resisted with vigorous consistency, the pursuit of science invariably appears to have been deprived of its solid foundation.[5]

Such a conviction about the connection between science and the truth of creation goes against two false ideas about the nature of science, one old and one more recent. The older error, embodied in Thomas Aquinas' great synthesis of Aristotle and Christianity, is the assumption that the universe has the sort of rationality which can be discerned by timeless and disembodied principles of thought. Empirical observation was irrelevant to a world where we "knew," with rational certainty, that (for example) heavenly bodies moved in perfect circles, or that projectiles moved in straight lines till attraction for their "natural" place overcame them, at which time they fell straight down, or that change did not take place beyond the orbit of the moon. Because it was assumed that our rationality corresponded to God's rationality, it was also assumed that we could, by thought alone, discern how creation operated. There was within this attitude little encouragement for actual observation and study of the created world. Thus the "truth of creation" was obscured, for truth was thought to reside in the timeless, uncreated principles to which creation (supposedly) had to conform, and the mind could find these out not necessarily by reference to creation itself, but by disciplined thought on first principles. So, brilliant as the Thomistic synthesis was, it did not provide notable encouragement for empirical science.

It was instead in the Franciscan theological and philosophical tradition, illustrated above by Bonaventure's words, that early science was nurtured. The Franciscans recovered the biblical truth that the most basic thing about God was his love, not his rationality. This put the emphasis on finding out what God has actually done, not what (according to our own reason) he ought have done (i.e., place the planets in perfectly circular orbits).

The other error about science is more recent. It is the positivist notion—perhaps most clearly set forth in the work of Ernest Mach—that scientific theories are simply convenient ways of organizing data: like telephone books or bus schedules. It is not the rationality or beauty of an explanation which is a clue to its truth, but simply its utility in accounting for all the data. "Scientists" in such a view, are not really necessary for science. Impersonal computing devices, registering, organizing and analysing the data, would theoretically do just as well. Science is, in fact, nothing more than the collection and organization of data.

At first glance such a view would seem to be more consistent with the truth of creation, i.e., add up the details, and truth will emerge. Its error is that it completely overlooks the element of personal passion, conviction, and response, what Michael Polanyi has so well described as "personal knowledge." That personal element brings the possibility of recognizing truth. As Polanyi has put it, "truth is something which can only be known by being believed."

But regarding the truth as personal does not destroy its objective character. As Polanyi puts it in the preface to his great work, the necessary personality of knowledge:

> ... does not make our understanding subjective. Comprehension is neither an arbitrary act nor a passive experience, but a responsible act claiming universal validity. Such knowledge is indeed objective in the sense of establishing contact with a hidden reality; a contact that is defined as the condition for anticipating an indeterminate range of yet known (and perhaps yet inconceivable) true implications. It seems reasonable to describe this fusion of the personal and the objective as Personal Knowledge.[6]

Two aspects of Polanyi's description say a great deal to us. The first is the fact that responsible science claims "universal validity." The idea that we "create our own reality" has no place in the laboratory, where repeatability is the fundamental test of the validity of a experiment (illustrated graphically a few years ago in the announcement of the achievement of "cold fusion"—and the later dismissal of the idea because of the unrepeatability of the experiment). The idea of repeatability suggests, then, a disciplined contact or dialogue with what Polanyi calls a "hidden reality" capable of yielding more truth. That sense of a "hidden reality" is what we are speaking of as the "truth of creation" as it nourishes science.

This characteristic of the created world—that its truth cannot be anticipated by mere thought, but must be investigated, reflects its contingency. That is, it depends for its reality on a will and act outside itself. Walter Thorson speaks eloquently of that contingency:

> ... we must not ignore the vigorous emphasis on the contingent

character of the natural order which was insisted on by the pioneers of science—as over against the concept of a necessary order derivable from (self-evident) principles of divine reason. This is the essential complement to the belief that a scientific theory may be entertained as potentially true, because it requires us to look outside ourselves to objective reality itself for validation (or falsification) of our ideas. These complementary ideas are opposite faces of the same coin. Nowadays we scientists take it for granted that theories must be tested against reality, but in the beginning it was not taken for granted. Moreover, a continuing awareness that order in nature is contingent (rather than rationally necessary or self-evident) is vital to the scientific enterprise...we have a sound theological basis for retaining a firm grasp on the concept of contingency: it reminds us that we are also creatures, and directs our attention to the reality outside us which God has made, as the sustaining support for our ideas.[7]

There is today a determined assault on the premise that science is a dialogue with a real world, irreducible to our notions about it. One of the sources of that assault is a mis-representation of the very personal nature of scientific discovery which Polanyi outlines so well. It was given influential articulation by Thomas Kuhn in his work, *The Structure of Scientific Revolutions*. Kuhn's major point is that science "advances" not by uncovering more truth about the universe, but simply by shifting from one paradigm to another because it is more useful. "We may," says Kuhn, "have to relinquish the notion, explicit or implicit, that changes of paradigm carry scientists and those who learn from them closer to the truth." He later elaborates that though we might speak of science evolving

...from primitive beginnings—nothing that has been or will be said makes it a process of evolution toward anything. Inevitably, that lacuna will have disturbed many readers. We are all deeply accustomed to seeing science as the one enterprise that draws constantly nearer to some goal set by nature in advance.[8]

Up to a point, Kuhn's analysis might be a helpful warning against a common kind of scientific hubris, a caution against thinking that our descriptions are ultimate, a reminder that in the created world there is always more mystery to be explored. Kuhn's analysis closes off that idea, however. Thus his work is ignored by every practising physical scientist I know of. They have no doubt at all they are engaged in the kind of investigation where the word "truth" is appropriate.

It is not the physical scientists, engaged in the difficult reading of the book of creation, who have popularized Kuhn's phrase "paradigm shift," but a whole range of other thinkers and writers whose distance from the created world allows them to speak as though truth were entirely a matter of our "paradigm" or "perspective." Real scientists, on the other hand, go on (in the words of Psalm 111) seeking out the "works of the Lord." Their belief in the truth of creation is an inseparable premise for their work, as it is for those of us who apply what they have learned (sometimes to our benefit, sometimes to our peril).

2. The truth of creation as the foundation of art

The word "creation" is the noun form of the Hebrew verb *bara* which is remarkable in the Old Testament for referring only to the acts of God. Greek cognates of the word likewise referred only to divine activity. This exclusive usage of words like "create," "creation" and "creativity" (in the sense of making from nothing) continued until the Renaissance. The first clear unequivocal usage of the word to describe human activity occurred in the sixteenth century. Its roots, however, are a few centuries earlier, in a recognition expressed brilliantly by Dante, that "art is the grandchild of God": that is, there is a profound analogy between the human ability (most dramatic in the work of various kinds of artists) to make new things, and God's creation out of nothing. Some recognition of this analogy seems to lie behind Bonaventure's thirteenth-century work, *On Retracing the Arts to Theology*.

The analogy between human creativity and divine creativity is a valid one, with far-reaching implications, as Dorothy Sayers has spelled them out in her book, *The Mind of the Maker*. At the same time, it is a dangerous analogy. Today the word "creation" is as apt to be applied to a painting, a movie, a dress style, or a dessert as it is to the work of God. From being applied only to the works of God the word now applies then, almost exclusively to human works.

The idea that art, as the supreme expression of human freedom, is a god-like activity, has reinforced several centuries of secularization, with very mixed results. The release of human creativity (and there is a proper use of the word) is an excellent thing, and it has resulted not only in great art, but in an accelerating development of technology. (It is worth remembering that the *techne* of "technology" is also the main word in Greek for "art.") But the danger in this recognition of human creativity is implicit in the high renaissance context of the birth of the idea. It is all too easy for a sinful human being to assume that his or her creativity is not so much a divine gift, but a sign that one is actually a kind of god, creating out of nothing, rather than embedded within a created world and living within its restraints. The artist (or for that matter the engineer) who sees himself as god is apt to forget the crucial fact that all human creativity is, in J.R.R. Tolkien's fine phrase, a kind of "sub-creativity." We make secondary worlds, but not the primary one. It is that primary world of sound, colour, form and texture which nourishes all the arts. The human "sub-creative" arts are always a dialogue with primary creation. Tolkien, whose language we are following here, has admirably described the relationship between primary and secondary worlds in his brilliant essay, "On Fairy Stories."

As the title suggests, he is writing in defence of fairy stories, or fantasy, which he regards as supreme examples of the sub-creator's art. But in so doing he recognizes the dependence of human creativity on divine creation:

> Fantasy is made out of the Primary World, but a good craftsman loves his material, and has a knowledge and feeling for clay, stone, and wood which only the art of making can give. By the forging of Gram cold iron was revealed; by the making of Pegasus horses were ennobled; in the Trees of the Sun and Moon root and stock, flower and fruit are manifested in glory. . . .It was in fairy-stories that I first divined the potency of the words and the wonder of the things: such as stone, and wood, and iron; tree and grass; house and fire; bread and wine.[9]

Or, as G. K. Chesterton puts it:

> … nursery tales only echo an almost pre-natal leap of interest and amazement. These tales say that apples were golden only to refresh the forgotten moment when we found that they were green. They

make rivers run with wine only to make us remember, for one wild moment, that they run with water.[10]

Both Tolkien and Chesterton are speaking of fantasy, a very specific kind of literary art. But in their defense of a kind of human creativity they defend also the overarching truth of creation. What they say of fantasy is true of all of the arts—and of every manifestation of human creativity. Human creative freedom flourishes when it is in dialogue with the primary realities of God's creation. So constrained—and so liberated—it is inexhaustible in its scope.

Sadly, human freedom and creativity have increasingly come to be understood not as a dialogue with, or enhancement of, primary creation—but as an affirmation of their independence from it. The idea is rooted in Romantic ideas of the artist as divine, perhaps best expressed in the work of William Blake. But the same idea has fed into the whole vast movement of modernity (against which Romanticism, ironically, is often seen to be a kind of reaction). Virginia Woolf, in advice to a painter, summed up the attitude succinctly: "Don't copy nature. One of the damn things is enough."

Nicholas Wolterstorff, in his work *Art in Action,* has carefully detailed this anti-creational tendency in the works of what he calls "the institution of high art." He traces carefully the process by which the expansion of the painter's centre of self-consciousness has come to be viewed as the absolutely central concern, in distinction from—and increasingly, in direct opposition to, any merely "mimetic" activity. In his words, "the basic image of the artist underlying modern Western art is that of the artist as a centre of consciousness who challenges God by seeking to create as God creates."[11]

Ultimately, as the sad progress of "modernism" in the arts has shown, the image of the artist as a kind of god creating his or her own world is ultimately destructive and empty, and leads to an ever-more frantic affirmation of one's own uniqueness. One of the major elements of "postmodernism" (and we must not forget that it was in speaking of the arts that the term was first used) has been to admit "nature" and "natural form" back into the arts. In a world where "value" has become increasingly drained of meaning and content by becoming merely subjective, "nature" or the world of creation has begun again to inform the work of the artist.

All of the arts flourish when they recognize that we are sub-creators within a primary world of created truth. The genuinely new things which the human artist can do are always to some extent derivative from creation and contingent upon it. The best human art is a kind of "gardening" of creation, a tending and keeping, a showing forth of what is given in that inexhaustible outpouring of good which we are calling the truth of creation. Cut off from that flow, the artist and her works wither.

3. The Truth of Creation as the Sustainer of Life

One need not agree with every argument of the "environmental movement" to affirm its basic premise: that we are nourished and sustained by a vast series of cosmic and planetary processes to which we interfere with our peril.

This relatively recent understanding of our place in an ancient cosmic and planetary drama bears a curious relationship to the other two senses of the truth of creation I have been describing in reference to science and art. On the one hand it is the result of (in old-fashioned language) creation's ability to convey information: it is the product of a detailed, patient, centuries-long "reading" of the book of creation, and thus a monumental witness to its truth and integrity. We can believe creation in what it says about itself. Thus the increasingly "seamless web" of causal explanation, from the first nanoseconds of the "cosmic fireball" through the details of stellar, chemical and biological evolution, down to our contemporary explorations of the astonishing architecture of DNA is in no sense a challenge to our belief in God the Creator, but a confirmation that (in the words of Psalm 111) "the works of the Lord are great."

Likewise it is the faithfulness of creation in the properties of matter—the conductivity of copper, the refractive qualities of glass, the explosive expansion of gases—which enables us to explore creation. We would know little (for example) of the protective ozone layer were it not for the accumulated humble acts of obedience to the truth of creation which we call "science" and "technology" (a word which, as we have seen, could also be translated "art").

But there is a darker side of this human ability to understand and manipulate creation. It is the modern tendency which we have already spoke of in the discussion of art, that is, the tendency to create a secondary human world which opposes or ignores the constraints and truths of primary creation. Examples are abundant and all too familiar. The spreading human world leaves little room for the habitats which support the staggering variety of living things. Thus we are living in one of the greatest periods of extinction of species that the world has ever seen. But it is not simply the spread of the human world which eliminates living room for other creatures. Even more insidious is our creation of tens of thousands of chemical substances which do not occur in "nature," that is, in primary creation. These substances cannot, in many cases, be taken up into the cycles of exchange which are such a marvellous provision for the purification of soil, air and water. Pesticides like DDT accumulate in the fatty tissues of higher predators, interfering with their fertility and thus garbling one aspect of the "truth" of creation. Chlorofluorocarbon molecules (CFC's)—the coolant often used in refrigerators and air conditioners—migrate into the upper atmosphere and function as a catalyst in the break-down of ozone. Radioactive wastes are being produced which have to be insulated from the rest of creation for many centuries. All of these secondary creations are in conflict with the life-giving truths of primary creation. Thus "the works of the Lord" are steadily diminished.

All this should not be taken as an argument against technology, which is an essential part of the human makeup, however. Artificial environments are as old as human civilization. We would do well, however to remember Jacques Ellul's observation in *The Meaning of the City* that the first builder of a city was Cain, and that the dynamic of city-building has always been to make a place where we could be invulnerable against all enemies, with no need to depend upon God.[12] One need not agree with all of Ellul's argument to grant that there has always been an element of un-health in our wish to be completely secure, to have things completely in our control. And so today, when more and more people live in an artificial environment, a "virtual world" which can be made more to our liking at the click of a "mouse," it is not surprising that we are increasingly cut off from the "truth of creation."

Perhaps the most spectacular example of our attempt to live in our own world is the fuel we use to keep it going. Primary creation, (at least on the planetary level) runs on energy "income"—the flux of solar energy which powers the winds and currents, and which, through photosynthesis, sustains all life. Human civilization, however, by contrast, is determined today to run not on energy "income," but to "burn up" the fossil reserves of coal oil and natural gas at a rate far greater than they were deposited. Quite apart from what this portends for future civilizations, it speaks of a determination to "do it our way," to step outside the truth of the self-sustaining cycles of creation and into a patched-together hovel of our own, which we maintain at ever greater cost (witness the danger and damage done by the West's determination to keep its supplies of cheap oil from the Middle East flowing).

Thus there is a profound anti-creational implication in human civilization. Loren Eisely described it well nearly 40 years ago:

> It is with the coming of man that a vast hole seems to open in nature, a vast black whirlpool spinning faster and faster, consuming flesh, stones, soil, minerals, sucking down the lightning, wrenching power from the atom, until the ancient sounds of nature are drowned in the cacophony of something which is no longer nature, something instead which is loose and knocking at the world's heart, something demonic and no longer planned—escaped, it may be—spewed out of nature, contending in a final giant's game against its master.[13]

Eisely uses the language of "nature." But it is, of course, creation that he is speaking of, and it is the truth of creation which is being first understood, then harnessed, then (the word is his) demonically denied in the construct of a human world with no room for "truths" other than the ones which we, the supermen, make for ourselves.

4. The Truth of Creation as News About the Creator

It is not surprising, in face of the various denials of the truth of creation which our civilization embodies, that many people today are turning, in a kind of thirsty desperation, to creation itself. Someone once remarked that to visit Mountain Equipment Co-op in Vancouver—or any one of similar purveyors of equipment for outdoor recreation (recreation: note the word), is to view the tip of a spiritual iceberg. Though there is a good deal of yuppie consumerism evident in the store (and many others like it, including the mother of all of them, Recreational Equipment Inc. in Seattle), there is an undertone of spiritual earnestness which makes this not just a clothing store and not merely a door to physical fitness. The determination to penetrate to the heart of the mystery of "nature"—whether through backpacking, or kayaking, or mountaineering, or through various kinds of appreciation of created things (bird-watching, wildlife photography, etc.)—is a spiritual quest. It is closely allied with "neo-paganism," interests in "native spirituality," and the ecofeminist honouring of Gaia, "goddess of the earth," and a number of other "new religious" accompaniments of postmodernism.

It would be easy (and not entirely incorrect) to dismiss these various creation-related spiritualities as simply the inveterate human tendency to worship the created instead of the Creator. But it would be a mistake to see only the idolatry in such movements. If indeed the truth of creation is evident to this present age, we need to recognize that, just as the tradition of science never left its meditation on that truth, and just as the arts need to continually return to it if they are to avoid absurdity and emptiness, so also the contemporary concern for the environment is a turning away from a civilization marked by a sterile artificiality, a spread of virtual realities which are neither reality or (in the fullest sense of the word) "virtual," to the one place where—particularly if the church will not speak—creation can be glimpsed. Lewis's words in defense of a "Romanticism" early in the century are just as apt today to describe these various glimpses of truth in creation:

> One of them [critics of "Romanti-cism"] described Romanticism as "spilled religion." I accept the description. And I agree that he who has religion ought not to spill it. But does it follow that he who finds it spilled should avert his eyes? How if there is a man to whom the bright drops on the floor are the beginning of a trail which, duly followed, will lead him in the end to taste the cup itself. How if no other trail, humanly speaking, were possible? [14]

Paul's sermons in the pagan world (at Lystra, in Acts 14, and at Athens, in Acts 17) contain great wisdom. The first thing he does is to recognize that they already know something of the Creator who he is proclaiming to them as Jesus the Christ: it is he who (through the cycles of creation) gives "rain from heavens, and fruit in season, and fills their hearts with joy." At Athens, Paul even quotes approvingly several of the pagan thinkers who express this recognition, including the one who said, "in him we live and move and have our being." But of course Paul does not stop at their confused recognition of an Unknown God glimpsed in creation; rather, he goes on to say, "he whom you ignorantly worship I am going to proclaim to you," and links that unknown God, which they had glimpsed through his truths in creation, to the crucified and risen Jesus Christ.

There is abundant biblical evidence of the "truth of creation." Perhaps the clearest biblical evidence is in Psalm 19:

> The heavens declare the glory of God; the skies proclaim the work of his hands. Day after day they pour forth speech; night after night they display knowledge. They have no speech, there are no words; [or, There is no speech or language where their voice is not heard]. Their voice goes out into all the earth, their words to the ends of the world.

The passage is significant for several reasons. Clearly, it says that the truth of creation has "gone out to the ends of the earth." There is no place (and, I think we can conclude, no time) where that message is not heard. Yet for all the power and scope of news about God which this passage describes, there is a curious incompleteness about that news. The incompleteness is reflected in widespread scholarly hesitation about how to translate verse 3, a disagreement which goes back through most of the history of English translations. The seventeenth-century King James rendering is "There is no speech or language where their voice is not heard," but the slightly older prayer book translation is "There is neither speech nor language, their voice is not heard." About half of subsequent English translations follow one reading, about half the other. The NIV translators opt for "there is no speech or language where their voice is not heard"—but keep the other rendering, "there is no speech, they have no words, no sound is heard from them" in a footnote.

The most literal—and, I think, the most likely—rendering of the verse is the starker "there is no speech, they have no words." The other reading is a possible construction, but seems to be put forth out of some embarrassed attempt to deliver the Hebrew text from its apparent contradiction. How could the heavens speak words and language in one verse, and have no speech or language in the adjacent verse? The problem is not trivial, and is highly significant for the question we are considering. How can creation be so full of truth (as we have tried sketchily to suggest in this paper), and yet so unheeded? Put the other way around, the Psalm points back to the problem I spoke of at the very beginning. How can mere "things" be true?; for truth involves will, purpose, commitment, someone standing apart from the things judged as true or false. Implicitly, the Psalm recognizes this, for it moves from the news about the wordless (though expressive) news of God in creation to the worded news about God in Scripture: "The law of the Lord is perfect, reviving the soul. The statutes of the Lord are trustworthy making wise the simple." And it ends with the familiar prayer that our own thoughts and words would be acceptable in the sight of our redeemer— and Creator.

The truth of creation is thus incomplete without the truth of Scripture. The words and language about the Creator which creation broadcasts are, in T.S. Eliot's words, "hints and guesses":

> For most of us there is only the unattended
>   Moment, the moment in and out of time,
> The distraction fit, lost in a shaft of sunlight,
>   The wild thyme unseen, or the winter lightning
> Or the waterfall, or music heard so deeply
>   That it is not heard at all, but you are the music
> While the music lasts. These are only hints and guesses....
>
> Hints followed by guesses; and the rest
>   Is prayer, observance, discipline, thought and action.
> The hint half guessed, the gift half understood, is
>   Incarnation....[15]

But hints can lead to the truth, and guesses can find the right answer. Let me close with two close-to-home examples of response, in an increasingly chaotic and superficial age, to the truth of creation.

Denise Levertov

The first is evident in the poetry of Denise Levertov, who for more than 40 years has been distinguished as one of the most articulate and morally courageous of American poets. (She was very involved in protests against the Vietnam war and went on to oppose nuclear weapons and militarism.) Levertov, from a Jewish background, and for most of her life an agnostic, has always been passionately troubled by the problem of innocent suffering, in both human and non-human creatures. Consider a recent work, "The Batterers":

A man sits by the bed
   of a woman he has beaten,
dresses her wounds, gingerly dabs at bruises,
Her blood pools about her,
   darkens.

Astonished, he finds he's begun to cherish her. He is terrified.
   Why has he never seen, before, what she was?
What if she stops breathing?

Earth, can we not love you unless we believe the end is near?
   Believe in your life unless we think you dying?[16]

In itself, this powerful elegy would fit within the general category of "ecofeminism." But for the past decade-and-a-half, Levertov's poems trace a journey beyond general grief at creation's degradation and back to the personal Creator hinted at in that grief. For when the grief draws back for a moment, Levertov finds there is also the urge to rejoice, and to worship—as she expresses in a little poem called "Of Being." The title suggests Heidegger. But Levertov is on a road which will lead far beyond Heidegger:

Of Being:
I know this happiness
   is provisional:
     the looming presences—
     great suffering, great fear—
        withdraw only
     into peripheral vision:
but ineluctable this shimmering
of wind in the blue leaves:
this flood of stillness
widening the lake of sky:
this need to dance,

this need to kneel:
        this mystery:[17]

Levertov is responding to the "truth of creation"—the totality of it. The punctuation which follows "this mystery" is not a period, but a colon, and includes the whole creation, the mystery that "there is anything at all." Her response is focussed, first into joy, in "this need to dance." But beyond that it is focussed into worship, "this need to kneel."

But Levertov was (at this time in her life) too honest a pagan to think that the truth which creation conveys was an invitation to worship creation. She followed the hints and guesses all the way to the Word made flesh in Jesus. The most remarkable of these many poems which record her slow conversion is the "Mass of St. Thomas Didymus," Thomas the doubter, the skeptic. The poem is too long to deal with carefully here, but it will reward careful reading by all late-twentieth-century Christians. Levertov has said that when she began the poem she was an agnostic, but that when she ended it, she was a Christian.

The poem is ordered under headings drawn from the Latin mass: Kyrie, Gloria, Sanctus, Credo, Benedictus, and Agnus Dei. At the beginning, its prayer addresses only "the deep, remote unknown": impersonal, still; yet Levertov prays to it "have mercy upon us."

The next section, Gloria begins with praise—mainly praise of things in creation: the wet snow; the "invisible sun burning beyond the white cold sky"; and finally, again, "the unknown." But now the unknown is acknowledged as "god or the gods" who

        imagined us. . .
            And gives us still
    in the shadow of death,
        our daily life.

The Credo begins, "I believe the earth exists." Yet it does not stop at the minimal declaration but continues:

and
in each minim mote
of its dust the holy
glow of thy candle.

108

Whose is the candle the "thy" refers to? Surely not the earth's. It is not simply creation she is addressing, but the truth of, in or behind creation. And Levertov is increasingly willing to address that Truth as a person.

Only in the fifth section, Benedictus, does the object of her emerging belief begin to be clear. She begins with a kind of salute to the spirit evident in creation, the spirit which (in the words of John the Baptist) is a kind of preparation (for, of course, the text of the "Benedictus" is John the Baptist's words: "Blessed is he who comes in the name of the Lord"):

Blessed is that which comes in the name of the spirit,
that which bears
the spirit within it.

The name of the spirit is written
in woodgrain, windripple, crystal,
in crystals of snow, in petal, leaf,
moss and moon, fossil and feather,

blood, bone, song, silence,
very word of very word, flesh and vision.

Then, after a long parenthesis agonizing over the problem of suffering,

But what of the deft infliction
upon the earth, upon the innocent of hell by human hands.

Is the word audible under or over
    this cacophony of violence?

Levertov continues, moving finally from bewilderment to awe to affirmation:

    But can the name
utter itself
    in the downspin of time?

Can it enter
   the void?

  Blessed
be the dust. From dust the world
utters itself. We have no other
hope, no knowledge.
            The word
chose to become
flesh. In the blur of flesh
we bow, baffled.

And in the *Agnus Dei*, the final section of the poem, Levertov finally, in worship to the cross-shaped centre of all creation, the centre of
Christian faith—and to the answer to her painful, lifelong questions
about suffering writes:

What terror lies concealed
in strangest words, *O Lamb*
of God that taketh away
the Sin of the World: an innocence
   smelling of ignorance,
    born in bloody snowdrifts.
God then,
encompassing all things is
defenceless? Omnipotence
has been tossed away, reduced
to a wisp of damp wool?[18]

Levertov's later poetry continues to express her passion for justice and
peace, her horror at cruelty and pain, and her openness to the beauty
and mystery of creation as vividly as ever. Yet the "Creator Spirit" is no
longer unknown, but recognized in Jesus, the truth of God in this present age. And her poems have become more explicit too about the
ambivalent human response to the truth of God manifest in creation,
the truth which is like a great waterfall. That image of the waterfall as a
ceaseless symbol in creation of the infinite mercy of God is central to the
passage I want to consider from my second contemporary writer, and so
I conclude this discussion of Levertov with a poem in which that mercy

110

and our often rejecting human response to it is also central:

> To live in the mercy of God.
> To feel vibrate the enraptured
>   waterfall flinging itself
>   unabating down and down
>   To clenched fists of rock
>
>   Swiftness of plunge,
>   hour after year after century,
>   O or Ah
>   uninterrupted, voice
>   many-stranded.
>   To breathe
>   spray. The smoke of it.
>   Arcs
> of steelwhite foam, glissades
> of fugitive jade barely perceptible. Such passion—rage or joy?
>
>   Thus, not mild, not temperate
> God's love for the world. Vast
> flood of mercy
>   Flung on resistance.[19]

Douglas Coupland

My concluding example of contemporary response to the "truth of God in creation" is perhaps in itself less conclusive, for the writer in question would not speak of himself as a Christian. Yet because he has become such an eloquent voice for "Generation X" (whose novel by that name popularized that label for—as he put it— "the first generation raised without religion"); because he speaks repeatedly both of God, and of the truth of creation which stands in such contrast to the shallowness of the West-coast, end-of-the century culture he so ruthlessly depicts; and because he is a fellow Vancouverite who is, I dare to hope, being drawn closer and closer to the God he longs for, I think he has much to say to us on the topic of this conference. I am speaking of course of Douglas Coupland, and in particular of his book, *Life After God*.

The physical appearance of that book conveys a self-deprecating message. Its boxy shape, big print, childish drawings and cover picture of a buddha-like toddler in a swimming pool all say: "Don't take me seriously." But in a culture of "contrived depthlessness" it is often the self-consciously shallow which conceals the greatest depth, and that is certainly the case with this work. Beneath its breezy mocking of a glossy Vancouver, it speaks with a Job-like eloquence.

The plot is thin. On the surface the book is little more than the first-person jottings of a thirty-something man in deep but loquacious depression, who grew up in comfort in North Vancouver. He describes his youth (now a decade-and-a-half behind him) like this:

As suburban children we floated at night in swimming pools the temperature of blood, pools the colour of Earth as seen from outer space. . . sometimes when we felt more isolated in our fetal stupor we would bump into each other in the deep end, like twins with whom we didn't even know we shared a womb.

Afterward we toweled off and drove in cars on roads that carved the mountain on which we lived…. The radio would be turned on, full of love songs and rock music; we believed the rock music but I don't think we believed in the love songs, either then or now. Ours was a life lived in paradise and thus it rendered any discussion of transcendental ideas pointless….

Life was charmed but without politics or religion. It was the life of children of the children of the pioneers—life after God—a life of earthly salvation on the edge of heaven.[20]

But bit by bit, this life in a post-God paradise has turned distinctly hellish. The narrator's casual marriage has ended; he no longer sees his wife and daughter. He has been on anti-depressant medication for weeks, sleeping on a sofa littered with yogurt containers and pizza boxes. He works for a software company, and after returning from a particularly depressing business trip to New York he stops taking his pills and drives on a whim on a rainy February day, to Horseshoe Bay, crosses to Vancouver Island, and passes through miles of clearcuts. He parks at the end of a logging road by uncut forest, and walks into the woods:

I saw massive Douglas firs that had fallen long ago—whales of biomass—the sky made solid—millennia worth of nutrients inhaled from the heavens now feeding bracket fungi and nursing rows of baby firs along their lengths. I tried to count one tree's rings but gave up back near the Dark Ages, before I could reach the Roman Empire or the birth of Jesus.[21]

And in a book entitled *Life After God*, the reference to giving up on counting tree rings which reach back to Jesus cannot be trivial.

He crawls into his tent:

… knowing that this is the end of some aspect of my life, but also a beginning—the beginning of some unknown secret that will reveal itself to me soon. All I need to do is ask and pray.[22]

He sleeps all night in the wet tent by the roaring water. In the morning, he walks down to the stream:

I peel my clothes and step into the pool beside the burbling stream, onto polished rocks, and water so clear that it seems that it might not even be there. My skin is grey, from lack of sun, from lack of bathing. And yes, the water is so cold, this water that only yesterday was locked as ice up on the mountaintops. But the pain from the cold is a pain that does not matter to me. I strip my pants, my shirt, my tie, my underwear and they lie strewn on the gravel bar next to my blanket.

And the water from the stream above me roars.

Oh, does it roar! Like a voice that knows only one message, only one truth—never-ending, like the clapping of hands and the cheers of the citizens upon the coronation of the king, the crowds of the inauguration, cheering for hope and for that one voice that will speak to them.[23]

"Like a voice that knows only one message, only one truth, never-ending...." Then in the book's penultimate paragraph comes the book's theme, the truth which has been unspoken through the whole novel, released now in the roar of a wilderness river:

Now—here is my secret: I tell it to you with an openness of heart that I doubt I shall ever achieve again, so I pray that you are in a quiet room as you hear these words. My secret is that I need God—that I am sick and can no longer make it alone. I need God to help me give, because I no longer seem to be capable of giving; to help me be kind, as I no longer seem capable of kindness; to help me love, as I seem beyond being able to love.[24]

This is not quite the record of a conversion. But it is nevertheless a truth about God carried by creation, a truth that we are creatures, that "we can no longer make it alone," that we need cleansing, salvation, wholeness. Listen to the book's conclusion:

I walk deeper and deeper into the rushing water. My testicles pull up into myself. The water enters my belly button and freezes my chest, my arms, my neck. It reaches my mouth, my nose, my ears and the roar is so loud, this roar, this clapping of hands.

These hands—the hands that heal; the hands that hold; the hands we desire because they are better than desire.

I submerge myself in the pool completely. I grab my knees and I forget gravity and I float within the pool and yet, even here, I hear the roar of water, the roar of clapping hands.

These hands—the hands that care, the hands that mold; the hands that touch the lips, the lips that speak the words—the words that tell us we are whole.[25]

In Christ and in Scripture God has given us more than hints and guesses. But for many people, and for many reasons, the truth of Scripture is at least temporarily closed. Not the least of these reasons is the way that the church has handled and lived out (or failed to live out) the truth of Scripture. In any case, we need ourselves to be open to the truth of creation; in science, in art, in our very biological life—and above all in the hints and guesses which pull us wordlessly to where the word is made flesh, to the one who said, "I am the way, the truth, and the life." And, open to that wordless utterance of the truth in creation, we need to be able to point others to the place where that truth has spoken decisively in Jesus.

C. S. Lewis, who has written as eloquently as anyone of the hints which creation carries of its Creator, puts the matter of the truth of creation in the proper perspective in a poem, with which I conclude:

Yes, you are always everywhere.
    But I,
Hunting in such immeasurable forests,
Could never bring the noble Hart
    to bay.

The scent was too perplexing for my hounds;
Nowhere sometimes, then again everywhere.
Other scents, too, seemed to them almost the same.

Therefore I turn my back on the unapproachable
Stars and horizons and all musical sounds,
Poetry itself and the winding stair of thought.

Leaving the forests where you are pursued in vain
—Often a mere white gleam—I turn instead
To the appointed place where you pursue.

Not in Nature, not even in Man, but in one
Particular Man, with a date, so tall, weighing
So much, talking Aramaic, having learned a trade;

Not in all food, not in all bread and wine
(Not, I mean, as my littleness requires)
    But this wine, this bread ... no beauty we could desire.)[26]

Endnotes

[1] Martin Heidegger, "The Origin of the Work of Art" in Albert Hofstadter, ed. *Poetry, Language, Thought* (New York: Harper and Row, Publishers, 1971), pp. 17-87.

[2] Michel Foucault, "Truth and Power" in The *Foucault Reader*, ed. Paul Rabinow (New York, Pantheon Books, 1984), p. 74. "'Truth' is linked in a circular relation with systems of power which produce and sustain it, and to effects of power which it induces and which extends [sic] it. A 'regime' of truth."

[3] R. Hooykas, *Religion and the Rise of Modern Science* (Grand Rapids: Eerdmans, 1972).

[4] St. Bonaventure, *The Soul's Journey Into God*, trans. Ewert Cousins (New York: Paulist Press) pp. 67-68.

[5] Stanley Jaki, *The Road of Science and the Ways to God* (Chicago: University of Chicago Press,

1978) p. vii

[6] Michael Polanyi, *Personal Knowledge* (Chicago: University of Chicago Press, 1958), p. vii.

[7] Walter Thorson, "Science as the Natural Philosophy of a Christian" *Journal of the American Scientific Affiliation* Vol. 33 number 2, June, 1981, p. 67.

[8] Thomas Kuhn, *The Structure of Scientific Revolutions, 2nd ed.* (Chicago: University of Chicago, 1970) pp. 170-171.

[9] J. R. R. Tolkien, "On Fairy Stories" *in Essays Presented to Charles Williams* (Grand Rapids: Eerdmans,) p. 76.

[10] G. K. Chesterton, *Orthodoxy* (New York: Image Books, n.d.) p. 54.

[11] Nicholas Wolterstorff, *Art in Action* (Grand Rapids: Eerdmans, 1980) p. 56.

[12] Jacques Ellul, *The Meaning of the City* (Grand Rapids: Eerdmans, 1970), ch. 1, "The Builders."

[13] Loren Eisely, *The Firmament of Time*

[14] C.S. Lewis, *Pilgrim's Regress* (Grand Rapids: Eerdmans, 1963), p. 11.

[15] T.S. Eliot, "The Dry Salvages" in *Four Quartets* (London: Faber, 1976) p. 44.

[16] Denise Levertov, "The Batterers" in *Evening Train*

[17] Levertov. "Of Being," *The Stream and the Sapphire* (New York: New Directions, 1997), p. 5.

[18] Denise Levertov, "The Mass of St. Thomas Didymus," in *Candles in Babylon* (New York: New Directions Press, 1982).

[19] DeniseLevertov, *The Stream and the Sapphire*, "To Live in the Mercy of God," pp. 31-32

[20] Douglas Coupland, *Life After God* (New York: Pocket Books, 1994), pp. 271-273.

[21] Coupland, p. 350.

[22] Coupland, p. 352.

[23] Coupland, p. 357.

[24] Coupland, p. 359.

[25] Coupland, p. 359.

[26] C.S. Lewis, "No Beauty We Could Desire" in *Poems* (New York: Harcourt, Brace, Jovonovich, 1964) p. 124.

6

Knowing Truth
in the Present Age

David Lyle Jeffrey

"Thirst was made for water; inquiry for truth."
——C.S. Lewis, *The Great Divorce*

"Send out thy light and thy truth, that they may lead me."
——Psalm 43:3

I have been asked by our hosts to address a difficult subject—too difficult by far for me. I shall therefore rely heavily on two sources which are more than sufficient: Holy Scripture and the congruent witness of the faithful Church. If what I have to say at length proves in any way unsound, the fault will to that extent be mine, and not that of my sources. Let me begin my recollection with a story.

In the next-to-last decade of the seventeenth century a certain priest of the Diocese of Ely, Robert Midgley by name, translated the celebrated *Morals* of the Greek biographer and philosopher Plutarch. The fourth and final volume bears a dedication to his Bishop, one Francis Turner, soon to be "removed" (1696). This volume has for its opening chapter one of Plutarch's most intriguing essays. It is entitled "Why the Oracles Cease to Give Answers." Briefly, the conclusion of the ancient author is, in the first instance, that it is because people stopped asking the oracle honest questions. Some grew impatient when the oracle didn't respond as they wished; still others would not stay for an answer. Eventually, he suggests, people thus conflicted in their motives came to forget about the oracles altogether; their priests were neither sustained nor replaced, the sanctuary became desolate, and at last it was inhabited by a fearsome dragon. To explain the demise of the institution it was generally said simply that "the oracles had ceased to give answers." The last excuse of the last faithful worshipers for not coming was fear of the dragon. "Yet," says Plutarch, "those that have written this did not well comprehend the occasion of the oracles ceasing; for the dragon did not make the place solitary, but rather, the solitude of the place occasioned the dragon to repair hither" (Trans. Robert Midgley [London, 1704], 9).

There are, of course, a number of possible applications for this story. Here is but one of them: Sometimes the denials we make of truth are really a product of our long absence from its oracle. Having learned to placate our consciences with a substitute for going there—a study of old reports, perhaps—then later becoming content with someone else's analysis and perhaps some reinterpretation of those old reports, we come at length to the point where it suffices for us to say that we, too, once visited the oracle in our youth. Now, of course, we have moved on to more immediate preoccupations. We put our current questions, self-serving as they are, to almost any other source. Even if the oracle should suddenly and miraculously proclaim truth loudly in our ear, or write it on the walls of our chamber, we would not recognize its proclamation as truth, but only, perhaps, as an unwelcome disturbance in the midst of our festivals.

Then suddenly, one day, judgment stands at the door.

I would like to make three basic points about knowing truth in the present age. Each is biblical. First: the recognition of truth depends in part upon the authenticity of one's intention to find truth: "Ask, and it shall be given you; seek and ye shall find. Knock and it shall be opened unto you" (Mt 7:7; Lk 11:9). Second: would-be discerners of truth must anticipate that now, as ever, truth will tend to be at odds with fashion (cf. 2 Pt 2:15-18). Third: coming to know what is theologically true when we meet it depends in large measure upon our already knowing that One who is Truth (Jn 14:6).

1. Recognition of Truth depends on a true intent to find it

The predicament we call postmodernity presents, I think, no fundamentally new problem to the Church. This, if only because attacks on truth—even the very possibility of truth—are as old as the blandishments of Eden's serpent, even though now they are in mode as the rhetoric in every contemporary courtroom and classroom in North America. Pascal, who died in 1662, can thus define both our problem and its only possible solution in terms which evoke the universal wisdom of Holy Scripture: "Truth," Pascal says, "is so obscure in these times, and falsehood so established, that unless we love the truth, we cannot know it" (*Pensées* 14.864).

On the other hand, when loving the truth is quite out of fashion, as it is at present, the very mention of the word can call up hatred. *Veritas otium parit*, said the Roman poet Terence—truth engenders hatred. The desire to flee truth is deep, deep in human nature, and that fact is not obscure to anyone. "How is it that to affirm the existence of truth seems to be tantamount to dogmatism and intolerance?" Jean (Cardinal) Daniélou asks this question in a fine little book called *The Scandal of Truth* (1962). Daniélou observes that when "nothing is less loved than truth," it is a certain sign that intelligence is in crisis—that people are not thinking straight. Usually there is an un-self-flattering reason for this.

St. Augustine, writing sixteen centuries earlier, brings us to consider how it is that the expression of hatred for the truth that we ought to love implies plainly that there is something other than truth that we must love more; and also, of course, that we see truth as an impediment to our indulgence in whatever, besides truth, we love.

> Why does truth call forth hatred? Why is Your servant treated as an enemy by those to whom he preaches the truth, if happiness is loved, which is simply joy in truth?

And then, as is often the case with Augustine, he answers his own question:

> Simply because truth is loved in such a way that those who love some other thing want it to be the truth, and precisely because they do not wish to be deceived, are unwilling to be convinced

119

that they are indeed deceived. Thus they hate the truth for the sake of that other thing which they love, because they take it for truth. They love truth when it enlightens them, they hate it when it accuses them. (*Confessions* 10.23)

What Augustine is getting at here, of course, is a fantasy in every age — the sinful, self-centered desire that "truth" should be subjective, individualistically defined. St. Thomas Aquinas makes the same point with reference to theological truth in particular. "We sometimes hate a particular truth when [we] wish that what is true were not true," says the great Doctor, and this reflex becomes particularly apparent when we "wish not to know the truth of faith, in order that [we] may sin freely" (*Summa Theologica* I-II, 29.5).

Old soldiers have a saying that, in war, truth is the first casualty. But surely this is the case with every kind of conflict, including inner and spiritual conflict. In all such cases we see that hatred of the truth begins not in fact with disbelief of the truth, but rather with a powerful desire to mask or rationalize appetites with which the truth is in evident conflict. Thus, as Nietzsche put it, "The most common lie is the lie one tells to oneself" (*Antichrist*, 55).

Every school child once used to know the story of a certain ancient who was said to have searched the world in vain for an honest man. (The story of Diogenes and his lantern is no longer part of the public curriculum.) But in the same vein, there is a notable passage in the book of the prophet Jeremiah which describes how a servant of the Lord might go looking in vain even for such a seeker as Diogenes:

Run ye to and fro through the streets of Jerusalem, and see now, and know, and seek in the broad places thereof, if ye can find a man, if there be any that executeth judgment, that seeketh the truth.... (Jer 5:1)

What most provokes him, says the Lord to his prophet, is the arrogant discrepancy between the hypocritical credal affirmations of religious men and the character of their actual belief and life: "Though they say, the Lord liveth, surely they swear falsely" (v. 2). This leads the prophet to a grief-stricken rejoinder:

O Lord, are not thine eyes upon the truth? Thou hast stricken them, but they have not grieved; thou hast consumed them, but they have refused to receive correction: they have made their faces harder than a rock; they have refused to return. Therefore I said, Surely these are poor; they are foolish: for they know not the way of the Lord, nor the judgment of their God.

I will get me unto the great men, and will speak unto them; for they have known the way of the Lord, and the judgment of their God—but these have altogether broken the yoke, and burst the bonds! (Jer 5:3-5)

The result for these "great" men — every one of whom, the text says, like an overfed horse, "neighed after his neighbor's wife" (v. 8) and whose house was "full of deceit" (v. 27) — is that they have lost the capacity for moral discernment and just judgment altogether.

Similar self-deceived repression of the truth occasions the apostles' warnings about apostate leadership in the last days of the Church, when:

men shall be lovers of their own selves, covetous, boasters, proud, blasphemers, disobedient to parents, unthankful, unholy, without natural affection, trucebreakers, false accusers, incontinent, fierce, despisers of those who are good, traitors, heady, highminded, lovers of pleasure more than lovers of God; Having a form of godliness, but denying the power thereof: from such turn away. For of this sort are they which creep into houses, and lead captive silly women laden with sins, led away with divers lusts, ever learning, and never able to come to a knowledge of the truth. (1 Tim 3:2-7)

Even when the truth is preached, says St. Paul, in such an age people will "turn away their ears from the truth, and shall be turned to fables" (2 Tim 4:4).

A similar warning about apostate churches in 2 Peter adds another dimension to the problem. This text suggests that, when such self-protecting motives are strong enough, subversion of the truth can become remarkably clever. Making reference back to Jeremiah's days, the epistle speaks of "false teachers" who through skillful redefinition and verbal sleight of hand insert into the doctrine of the Church "damnable heresies" by means of which many will be deceived and even "the way of truth" shall be represented as an evil. By feigned words and clever rhetoric they will make the truth itself to seem a lie (2:1-3).

In our own age we can confirm that deliberate theological error seldom lacks for sophisticated articulation. Indeed, an apparent liberality of spirit and cleverness with words is often the hallmark of those who hate the truth. This can develop to the degree that, as St. Peter suggests in his letter (citing the case of Balaam the prophet [Num 22]), even a dumb ass may more likely speak the truth than the official prophets (2 Pet 2:15-21).

This doesn't mean, mind you, that misguided prophets don't have a lot to say; it is often the case that they seem more voluble than anyone else. Kierkegaard thought that "talkativeness," in fact, was a good indicator of the sterility of one's spiritual life, and that pseudo-intellectual talkativeness was a certain sign of it (*Present Age*, 68-69). Such wordy would-be-revolutionaries in the Church, for Kierkegaard, are to be expected to try to effect a dissociation between truth and the intellect. Intelligent people, they are most likely to pretend, are the ones whose superior enlightenment recognizes no such thing as objective truth. Capital "T" truth, they will sneer, is fodder for donkeys. But amongst themselves they will say, "look—if we don't want the donkeys to get angry and buck us off the saddle then we must try to anesthetize them with ambiguous verbiage, as well as by employing other shrewd means of subverting their resistance." These strategies, to which whole courses are devoted in our seminaries, have the added advantage of providing further opportunities for cleverness. But as Oscar Wilde suggests ironically, in his essay "The Decay of Lying," when put into practice in the parish, such cleverness can nonetheless appear to the common layman as asininity:

> ... In the English Church a man succeeds, not through his capacity for belief, but through his capacity for disbelief. Ours is the only Church where the sceptic stands at the altar, and where St. Thomas is regarded as the ideal apostle. Many a worthy clergyman, who passes his life in admirable works of kindly charity, lives and dies unnoticed and unknown; but it is sufficient for some shallow uneducated passman out of either University to get up in his pulpit and express his doubts about Noah's ark, or Balaam's ass, or Jonah and the whale, for half of London to flock to hear

him, and to sit open-mouthed in rapt admiration at his superb intellect....

That Wilde intends a rebuke to the pew as much as the pulpit is, of course, clear, just as, with a more virtuous intent, did St. Peter in his catholic epistle. Both say that truth would not be so often hidden from view if so many of us were not so responsive to having our ears tickled, content to receive a humorous placebo instead of the medicine we need.

It would be a mistake to think that truth-denying postmodernists never themselves assert anything as true. Indeed, the determination to assert as "truth" what cannot be supported in fact has become a poisonous epidemic in academic and religious institutions in our time. A favourite target is, unsurprisingly, saints of the Church and distinguished Christians. Thus, the *Cambridge Encyclopedia of English Literature* calls, without a shred of evidence whatsoever, two eminent Christians of the fourteenth century—both Wycliffites, and one a Christian poet (Sir John Clanvowe)—homosexual lovers. Similar claims, without foundation in evidence whatsoever, are made when convenient about biblical characters such as David and Jonathan or against major theologians of the historic Church. The people who make these kinds of assertions may well be prompted by vested interest—of that it is difficult to judge, but the consequences of such fabrications are readily apparent: the vast majority of faithful Christians who read these falsifications find them painfully disorienting, while the enemies of the Gospel find them simply "amusing" and, of course, conveniently self-serving.

So what can we do to recover for ourselves a clearer sense of the actual character of truth? Here is one suggestion: we need to do a much better job of cultivating Christian intelligence. To begin with, we need to stop confusing intelligence with levels of formal "education." As innumerable current events make clear, there is no necessary connection between intellectual capacity (or training) and moral intelligence. Indeed, with respect to moral or spiritual realism there seems just now to be an inverse correlation in many quarters. In his remarkable parable, *The Great Divorce*, C.S. Lewis captures admirably the actual relationship between truth and intelligence as we find it in the teaching of Scripture and in the persistent understanding of the Church. In Lewis's parable, you may remember, theologians and bishops do not come off any better than the rest of us. We find that intellectual attainment is no guarantee of access to truth whatsoever, that education (including theological education) often serves simply to multiply the strategies for subversion and evasion. But such evasion, of course, does not change the nature of truth any more than it models a proper use of the intellect. What Scripture, the Church, and individual Christian experience teach us, as Fr. Daniélou so nicely puts it, is that, whatever else men may pretend,

> there is an order of the real where things are ranged hierarchically according to their density of existence, their weight, what St. Augustine called *auctoritas*. Truth consists in the intelligence's conforming itself to this order. Being intelligent means simply that. Intelligence does not consist in the more or less brilliant performance of the mind. No, it consists in knowing reality as it is. That is why for the Bible being intelligent means recognizing the sovereign reality of God. Who but "the fool says in his heart: There is no God" (Ps 13:1)? This is the complete reverse of what modern man calls intelligence. For in the biblical view a great intellectual may be perfectly stupid, and some poor uneducated woman praying in a church infinitely more "intelligent" than he. (*The Scandal of Truth*, 8)

II. Discernment of truth must anticipate that truth will typically be at odds with fashion

Reality is one thing; the ideas and judgments by which we think about reality are another. The first is objective, the second subjective. Yet in the present age these two are increasingly conflated. This is particularly the case with impressionistic and, as we like to say, "theoretical" religious discourse.

The phenomenologists are certainly right about one aspect of this subjectivity. We tend to find (or invent) what we are looking for. And what we are looking for, though we hate to admit it, is seldom the truth. Why is this? Well, as Scripture, the teaching of the Church, and experience all make clear, it is often because we tend to prefer self-justification, a rationalization for something for which we have an ardour more intense than we feel for truth, and which truth seems to threaten. But what Scripture tells us is that in this as in any other age what will follow from a general attempt to exchange the truth of God for a lie is a kind of ludicrous anti-realism which is destructive, and in which a lot of people will get hurt. Eventually the lie makes fools of those who choose it, even though for a time the whole culture chooses it with them and they feel secure in the safety of numbers. We should perhaps remind ourselves that a certain northern rodent also takes its bearing from where the crowd is moving, and tends not to notice until too late that the crowd has thinned out rather precipitately.

Samuel Johnson, the great essayist and dictionary-maker of the eighteenth century, gets at St. Paul's point in a slightly different way: "Truth sir," said Johnson, "is a cow; which, when skeptics have found it will give them no more milk, they have gone off to milk the bull." Milking the bull, as Johnson's audience knew, is not only futile but positively dangerous to one's health. Johnson expected skeptics of revealed truth thus to be corrected by the power of barnyard reality more quickly than did Wilde; by the 1890s, bull-wallop was for most people just a figure of speech. By the 1990s it has become, at every possible level, a kind of staple in our cultural diet. "Infotainment" is another word for it. You can get yours on the Net, on TV, or in the ubiquitous tabloids. You can also get it in some more formal and "churchy" environments. You know the headlines from your grocery shopping: "Bigfoot Got my Sweetheart," "Chocaholic Mom gives birth to Sugar-Coated Baby," "Church Organist Inseminated by UFO Aliens, Gives Birth to new Primate." Etc. (Okay, I confess: I made that last one up.) A feature article in the *Ottawa Citizen* recently (January 4, 1998) characterized the tabloid as the exemplary postmodern phenomenon. Nietzsche's dictum that "there are no facts; the true world has in the end become a fable" may be almost perfectly realized in this popular medium. Articles which claim the preposterous as true are, according to Eddie Clontz, Editor-in-chief of *The Weekly World News*, just a popular application of the same postmodern theory that more or less equally characterizes politics, preaching, and the academy: "People rewrite history all the time," he says, "and so do we." In his stable are a completely fictitious corps of doctors and scientists of obscure origins, complete with "scholarly looking headshots." On-line editor Cynthia Rigg refers to a cadre of fictitious "Bible scholars" who have been "used over and over again by the tabloid, and are now quite respected." And of course there are always a few mostly warm bodies from the Jesus Seminar or ecclesiastical offices closer to home when their creativity falters. Yet according to repeated surveys, 40% of the millions who regularly read these rags believe their stories to be true.

What is truth? What is the truth of hypnotically induced "memories" in an environment where it is the victimization *du jour* to "discover" the most sordid sort of abuse under every gesture of parental affection or constraint? What is the truth preserved in legal judgments based on a perceived need to "correct social imbalances" or to "empower" some groups at the expense of others, abusing where necessary fact and accountability? What is the justice which ensues in legal judgments formulated on such fabrications? What is the value of scholarly findings or exegesis of texts based upon raw advocacy rather than an intention to understand what is actually there? If the truth of the matter isn't what we want to hear, does it really matter so much if we get a social construct—or vivid invention—in its place? After all, as Oscar Wilde would say, the lie is often more "interesting." What makes it interesting may be that it gives temporary advantage to the will to power over the will to truth, though this is seldom admitted. But this motive is surely there, prompting hatred for the notion of an objective truth, for truth that by definition must be true for you just as it is true for me.

In this light we can begin to see why truth is seldom fashionable. The illusion so cherished by people of all ages, so apparent already in the serpent's tempting in Eden, is an illusion of anarchic self-empowerment achieved by denying the truth. We shall be as gods, we think, able to decree for ourselves what is to be evil and what is to be good. This allure, so transparent in the Genesis account of our fallen nature, is what continues to make the impulse to hubristic anti-realism so irresistible—and so dangerous. For "rejecting objective truth amounts to a subtle willingness to set my face against God." Conversely, "acknowledging what is, submitting to the real [such as, e.g., the reality of Creation], means acknowledging something I have not decided for myself and therefore already saying yes to God" (Daniélou, 13).

There is, therefore, much at stake in what I am here calling "fashion" and what the Bible typically calls "worldliness." It is not to the credit of Western Christianity that we have made so many ardent and repeated accommodations to fashion, courting the gods of the marketplace.

Much of what is essential to the truth of the Gospel has been sacrificed to our desire not to seem too different from our contemporaries—much more than the truth can afford. What Kierkegaard said about this tension more than a century-and-a-half ago still holds:

> The true must essentially be regarded as in conflict with this world; the world has never been so good, and will never become so good, that the majority will desire the truth, or have the true conception of it in such a way that its proclamation must consequently immediately gain the support of everyone. No, he who will proclaim some truth in truth, must prepare himself in some other way than by the help of such a foolish expectation; he must be willing essentially to relinquish the immediate. (*Works of Love*, 2.10)

Willingness to relinquish the immediate, even if the immediate is preferment in what C.S. Lewis called the "inner ring" of popularity, or just the acceptance most of us would some days be grateful for a little more of, is indispensible to our discernment of the truth.

As Christians we are called to be a "sign of contradiction" to our age by the One who endured such "contradiction of sinners against himself" (Heb 12:3). Contradiction of fashion, so far from being bad for us, is essential to our spiritual health and thus to the integrity of any witness we might hope to have. For the Christian, "abolition of the principle of contradiction, expressed in terms of existence, means to live in contradiction with oneself," as Kierkegaard says (*Present Age*, 68). So much is this so that "knowing truth in the present age" is pretty much impossible if we are unwilling to be known as a sign of contradiction to the age, or unwilling to learn to let our yea be Yea and our nay, Nay. As St. Basil (in his *On The Holy Spirit*) once said, "Yea and nay are but two syllables, yet there is often involved in these little words at once the best of all good things: Truth, and that beyond which wickedness cannot go, a Lie" (1.2). As with much else we learn in life, often sorrowfully, in truth there is no "yes" without a corresponding "no."

III. Knowing truth when we meet it depends greatly upon already knowing the One who is Truth

"What is truth?" When Pilate asked his question he was the one, of course, already under conviction. The prisoner brought before him, bound in fetters, had seared the conscience of his inquisitor with an invisible sword. It divided asunder the thoughts and intentions of Pilate's heart, and he felt the oppressive weight of his own far more heavy (though invisible) shackles. Pilate's kingdom was strictly of this world, and to its temporizing venality he was himself a prisoner. Which is to say, he lived by lies, by the maintenance of politic and fashionable institutional fictions. And yet, when Jesus said to him, "Every one who is of the truth heareth my voice" (Jn 18:37), his professional composure was evidently pricked. The evidence is not only that he asked his peremptory, skeptical and parrying question, but that he refused to stay for an answer. He did tell the accusers of our Lord: "I find in him no fault at all." What he did not say, unsurprisingly, was whether he was beginning to note fault anywhere else.

A profound irony in Pilate's question to Jesus has often been noted. His evasive skepticism concerning the very possibility of truth in a world where men customarily live by lies had led him to a common category mistake. "What is truth?" he asks, as though truth were a chimerical abstraction. Pilate's question is rhetorical; it presumes the impossibility of a coherent answer. Yet the One of whom it is mockingly asked is, John's Gospel shows us, not less than Truth himself, the only One who has ever been able to say "I am the Way, the Truth, and the Life" (Jn 14:6). Had Pilate but recognized him, known him for who he is, he would have "heard his voice" and thus at least reformulated his inquisition: "*Who* is Truth?" But that is a question a faithful person alone will ask—"every one who is of the truth." Whoever evades the absolute character of Truth will miss him.

Have you noticed how often it is in Scripture that the mention of God's truth ('*emeth*) is coupled with righteousness (*zedekah*)? In the Song of Moses the prophetic poet sings, "He is the Rock, his Word is perfect: for all his ways are judgment; a God of truth and without iniquity, just and right is he" (Dt 32:4). It is the righteous nation which keeps the truth (Is 26:2); indeed, "he who speaks the truth," says the book of Proverbs, "exemplifies righteousness" (Prv 12:17). And who among us can read these lines of the Psalmist without being provoked to repentance:

Lord, who shall abide in thy tabernacle? Who shall dwell in thy holy hill? He that walketh uprightly, and worketh righteousness, and speaketh the truth in his heart. (Psalm 15:2)

If the petitioner after truth is sincere, that is to say, striving after righteousness, then he will not shy away from the persistent connection Scripture makes between truth and judgment, the judgment—we might say the justice—of God. "I have chosen the way of truth," says the Psalmist, and as a consequence, "thy judgments have I laid before me" (Ps 119:30). "Thy Law is the truth," he writes later in the same poem, "thy commandments are truth" (119:142, 151). If we want to come to a knowledge of the truth, say the writers of Scripture everywhere, then we will have to get into the habit of doing the truth, for that is the only way we can learn to recognize the Author of Truth when he speaks to us or shows us the power of his hand. "These are the things that ye shall do," says the prophet Zechariah, "speak ye every man the truth to his neighbour; execute the judgment of truth and peace in your gates" (8:16), and St. Paul, echoing him, makes this way of living with each other a demonstrative consequence of our imitating "the truth as it is in Jesus," of our putting on the new man "which after God is created in righteousness and true holiness" (Eph 4:21-25).

When we are careful to speak the truth to our neighbour, our will to truth in principle is strengthened in a manner analogous to the way in which it is strengthened by our carefulness to be honest in our self-examination before God. (The New Testament term is *aletheia*, both veracity and rectitude.) This is what St. Anselm of Canterbury has in mind in his treatise *On Truth* when he says that truth in the will—"truthfulness in the inward parts" (Ps 51:6)—is, properly speaking, identical to that correctness of the will which we call uprightness (*rectitudo*)" (*De Veritate*, 4). It is this reciprocity of rectitude and truth which makes it impossible that anyone should know the truth who does not love Truth, or that anyone should love the truth who does not live it. Doing what truth teaches is "telling the truth," while acting in a way contrary to truth is precisely equivalent to telling a lie (*De Veritate*, 9). This is why St. Paul, in Romans 1, can be so categorical when he says that God's judgment falls hard upon those who "hold the truth in unrighteousness" (Rom 1:18). It is entirely possible for someone to mouth the very words of scriptural truth and, in the context of their mouthing, to change the truth of God into a lie (v. 25). And this happens especially when those who, though professing themselves to be wise, in their rejection of revelation and the authority of objective truth, reveal themselves to be fools (Rom 1:22).

I do not pretend that these are not hard words. (I certainly do not find them easy to speak.)

None of us, I think, sets out to become a fool. Foolishness rather comes to us by degrees, as the sodden fruit of a process of self-deception. A lie, repeated often enough, gets to be taken for the truth—first by the one who convinces himself of it, subsequently by others who hear it over and over again and forbear to check on the facts. Conversely, the truth, perhaps repeated often but without being grounded in the love and life of that truth, becomes a living lie in the making. That is what Romans 1 teaches us and it makes for the most disastrous of all follies. Yet all the while it too remains correctable by a check for correspondence with the facts of a given life.

This notion of how we may come to know truth pertains most closely both to common sense and to older philosophical theories of truth: there ought to be a correspondence between a proposition (or claim) and a fact or state of affairs that verifies it. The biblical notion of truth bears less relation to the philosophers' more academic notion of verification by coherence (as in the coherence among propositions), simply because the normative character of Scripture grounds all truth in history and revelation. But with the third and now perhaps most common academic definition of truth, that of the pragmatists, biblical truth has nothing in common at all. In pragmatic theory truth is to be defined in terms of its satisfactoriness—i.e., whether in our own social or political circumstances it "works." For William James "true ideas are the ones we can assimilate" (*Pragmatism*, 6)—that is to say, the criterion of truth is finally its locatability in the "comfort zone" of the knower. Alas, this is precisely the sort of dissociation from reality which corrupts the idea of objective truth altogether.

Of the three principal definitions of truth propounded by philosophers through the ages—correspondence, coherence, and pragmatic—correspondence is then the one clearly favoured by the writers of Scripture. This correspondence is, of course, of words to facts—to the facts of the Gospel, e.g., the atoning death and resurrection of Jesus. It is also in a correspondence of word to life. Scriptural truth is also manifest, therefore, as opposition to falsehood and hypocrisy, as in Jesus' rebuke of the Pharisees, who loved the letter of the law but not its higher purpose, and of the Sadducees, who denied the power of the resurrection. Finally, truth in Scripture is the content of what we believe, guaranteed by the very character of God himself, and of Jesus who is the Truth of God revealed to us. His *troth*, his fidelity to his promises from the beginning of the world, is our guarantee of every other truth, and it is the standard by which, finally, we are able to say what truth is.

In the New Testament, Peter spoke for all of us in the Church when he asked and answered a rhetorical question: "Lord, to whom shall we go? Thou hast the words of eternal life. And we believe and are sure that thou art the Christ, the Son of the living God" (Jn 6:68-69). Peter's answer corresponds to what he has come to know personally about Jesus. These phrases become the apostolic words of truth, and, as the substance of holy conversation in the Church (1 Pt 1), they make it possible for the Church to be an oracle which answers still, to be as Paul has it, "the house of God, which is the church of the living God, the pillar and ground of the truth" (1 Tm 3:15).

When the Church is in love with Jesus, then it knows the ground of Truth: "And hereby do we know that we know him," says St. John in his first pastoral letter, "if we keep his commandments. He that saith, I know him, and keepeth not his commandments, is a liar, and the truth is not in him" (1 Jn 2:3-4). Holiness is a matter of practising the truth and a matter of knowing the one who is Truth: "Who is a liar," he continues, "but he that denieth that Jesus is the Christ? He is antichrist, that denieth the Father and the Son" (1 Jn 2:22). It is impossible to be holy without a living belief in this Truth. Indeed, it is impossible to be Christian without a living belief in this truth.

Of course, these are unfashionable words. They are not our words. The question is: how can we know their truth in such times? Well, Scripture says, by loving that One who is timeless Truth, and by paying him heed according to his word. His Word is truth, and we will know him in his word, says the beloved disciple, if we live out the truth of his word, not only by a love which is a matter of words, but "in deed and in truth." For, John says, this is the way in which we know that we are of the truth," and "assure our hearts before him" (1 Jn 3:18-19).

When we live thus in his truth we are of God, and all those who know God, he says, will give us a hearing. Conversely, whoever does not belong to God will not give us a hearing. Yet even their antagonism is not without value to us with respect to our knowing the truth, for, when we are living in faithful obedience to the One who is Truth, then such antagonism can actually confirm us in our certainty: "Hereby know we the spirit of truth, and the spirit of error" (1 Jn 4:6). And blessed are we, after all, when men revile us for his name's sake" (Mt 5:11).

It is crucial to know which spirit is which, since we too shall be judged. Discerning the spirits, as John's first letter encourages, is a necessary task because "many false prophets are gone out into the world" (1 Jn 4:1) and their falseness is directed at a diminishment of Christ. But the purpose of our discernment is not in the first instance to win arguments or political battles with such people. Nor do we seek it as a means of self-justification. It can be, after all, rather easy to identify fault and to name it; and if we are not prayerful, the manner in which we conduct our "trying the spirits, whether they are of God" may open us up to the greater judgment. The trick is to learn to tell the truth which is necessary (not more) without forgetting to live in the light of the Truth while telling it.

When it comes to the extreme case of someone who, while bearing the authority of the Church, willfully misleads others, then we may have little choice but to declare against that lie such truth as we ourselves have been willing to live by. But then we ought to speak only of what we know in that most thorough sense of knowing—the holy conversation of our life in him who alone is Truth. We will be most true to him when we speak least for ourselves and perhaps, on some occasions, remain prayerfully silent.

If it is our lot to have to fight the Dragon—and it will not be our lot unless we have unarguably been chosen for it—then we need to be very sure that we have been equipped for this terrible task. "His truth shall be [our] shield and buckler," says the Psalmist (91:4), and St. Paul adds that against "the rulers of the darkness of this world, against spiritual wickedness in high places" we will need the "whole armour of God." But you and I will want to remember that the foundation of that armour, first on the apostle's list, is that we should have our "loins girt about with truth," and that we should be wearing with it "the breastplate of righteousness" (Eph 6:11-16).

So then, let each of us consider carefully what Augustine says in his commentary on John 14:6: "every true man is true from the Truth .... The Truth, then, cannot speak contrary to the true man, or the true man contrary to the Truth" (in *Joan. Ev.* 5:1). That is the "correspondence" for which each of us must daily pray: that we may come to know him who is the ground of all Truth, and so to have, in such measure as is possible for us, more of his mind about all these things.

www.ingramcontent.com/pod-product-compliance
Lightning Source LLC
Chambersburg PA
CBHW032104080426
42733CB00006B/406